PRAISE FOR
AND *THE CARIN*

"We all work in an increasingly competitive environment and need every edge to get ahead and stay ahead. TJ's eloquent Caring Warrior *provides a straightforward guide to more effectively engage your teams and maximize results. It's a book you'll want to read more than once and to pass on to your colleagues who really care about their people. I've had the distinct privilege of working with TJ, and I know that what he outlines really works!"*

—Mark McDade, chief operating officer, UCB

"*Are you a Caring Warrior? Someone who leads with his or her heart and cares deeply about others? TJ Jones is a Caring Warrior at home, at work, and in the community, and he is passionate about creating the next generation of Caring Warriors…and God knows this country really needs it. TJ has a lifetime of experience teaching leaders how to be Caring Warriors, and he shares those experiences with us and gives a road map to implement it in our own lives. If you read and apply the principles in this book, you will become a more productive leader at work and at home. I highly recommend this book to anyone who leads or wants to lead a team and become more effective doing it."*

—Steve Cesari, best-selling author, *Clarity: How to Get It, How to Keep It & How to Use It to Balance Your Life*

THE
CARING
WARRIOR

AWAKEN YOUR POWER TO
LEAD, INFLUENCE, AND INSPIRE

T. J. JONES

Advantage®

Published by Advantage, Charleston, South Carolina.
Member of Advantage Media Group.

ADVANTAGE is a registered trademark, and the Advantage colophon is a trademark of Advantage Media Group, Inc.

Printed in the United States of America.

ISBN: 978-1-59932-760-0
LCCN: 2016956130

Cover design by Katie Biondo.

This publication is designed to provide accurate and authoritative information in regard to the subject matter covered. It is sold with the understanding that the publisher is not engaged in rendering legal, accounting, or other professional services. If legal advice or other expert assistance is required, the services of a competent professional person should be sought.

 Advantage Media Group is proud to be a part of the Tree Neutral® program. Tree Neutral offsets the number of trees consumed in the production and printing of this book by taking proactive steps such as planting trees in direct proportion to the number of trees used to print books. To learn more about Tree Neutral, please visit **www.treeneutral.com.**

Advantage Media Group is a publisher of business, self-improvement, and professional development books. We help entrepreneurs, business leaders, and professionals share their Stories, Passion, and Knowledge to help others Learn & Grow. Do you have a manuscript or book idea that you would like us to consider for publishing? Please visit **advantagefamily.com** or call **1.866.775.1696.**

For Molly, my angel. You make everything possible. I love you.

"I am a fragment of a mirror whose whole design and shape I do not know. Nevertheless, with what I have, I can reflect light into the dark places of this world—into the black places in the hearts of men—and change some things in some people. Perhaps others may see and do likewise. This is what I am about. This is the meaning of my life."

—Robert Fulghum, *It Was On Fire When I Lay Down On It*

INTRODUCTION

Kneeling in the mulch behind my house, I burst into tears. Sobs. Shock. My heart rate jumped. I was shaking. I felt panicked and out of control. *Where is this coming from? What the hell is wrong with me?*

The sound of a motor jolted me out of my moment. My neighbor Charlie was coming around the back corner of my house on his souped-up John Deere riding mower. I quickly caught my breath and wiped my face with my sleeve. My wife and kids were away for the day. Thank God it was Charlie. He was the ideal neighborhood friend: kind, calm, and unassuming. He must have noticed that something was off with me, but he simply smiled and asked if I needed help with anything. I remember feeling grateful that he showed up when he did, although we never spoke of it.

Why was I in this state? And how did I get there? Looking back now, with a few years of perspective, I can see that my spirits had been on a downward slide for a quite a while. I was grieving the losses of my stepfather and biological father, both of whom had recently died. We had moved, and I was constantly on the road for work, logging in over 150 nights per year. Like many midlife and midcareer women and men, I had reached a physical, mental, and emotional burnout. Of course there had been many blessings: marriage, four children, promotions and awards, recognition and trips, more money, and expanding responsibilities with industry leaders and start-ups. But in spite of outside appearances, I was very unhappy. I was unable to see all the light in my life. I was miserable, and my work situation had picked the scab off my deeper wounds.

Work began for me as a high school English teacher and football coach, which I loved. But I could barely make ends meet, so I got a job as a salesman in New York City. I told the hiring manager, Manny, "If I can get teenagers excited about Shakespeare, I can sell your products." He gave me a chance at a new career in the Big Apple. I come from the idyllic small town of Livonia, which is in the Finger Lakes region of upstate New York. Navigating a new career in the big city was quite a challenge, but I moved through the ranks and into a variety of sales and leadership roles, eventually becoming head of training and leadership development. With the help of a great team, I emceed national meetings, created learning content, and directed all leadership development and training. I also worked with human resources on leadership assessments, executive-coaching initiatives, management-candidate programs, and company culture. I never lost the idealism of the teacher. I was always most passionate about the people side of work, so I naturally assumed and welcomed the role of life-and-career coach to many employees and colleagues at every level. My experiences were like an advanced degree in self-help, organizational behavior, and leadership studies.

In a twenty-year career, I had eighteen different bosses. The companies I was part of were acquired on eight separate occasions, so along with different colleagues and teams, I experienced at least eight senior leadership (and thus, culture) changes. As the organizational changes piled up, my spirit eroded, and my cynicism and disillusionment swelled. Cheerleading each time for the "new reality" through all the uncertainty, when I too had fears and uncertainties, was exhausting—like lost sleep you never catch up on.

We all know that change is a necessary part of the journey, particularly in the business world. But it feels personal. As I see it, *all change is personal*. We're human beings with feelings. We suffer. We worry. We want to feel safe and trusting. We want to feel valued and validated. We want to feel strong enough to navigate the journey. We want to be handled with humanity and integrity. We want to be cared about.

By the time the last acquisition was upon me, I wasn't in the mood, and I didn't experience much caring from the new owners. I took it all personally. Because I was in a leadership role, I sat in on personnel discussions. Individuals were spoken about disrespectfully, their lives and careers tossed around like trading cards. Those of us who would be asked to stay on after this latest deal closed would have to prove ourselves yet again and accept another new culture, one in which we felt unsafe. The banter in these meetings was often unprofessional and mean spirited. I remember thinking that the bullies had taken over the playground, and I resented it.

After the deal closed, there was no honeymoon phase. My new boss railed me for being too nice to my people and suggested that the leadership team didn't respect me. I had never heard those words before in my life, nor have I since. Not only did those words hurt, but they also fueled my anger and resentment. I don't have much of a poker face, so I'm sure my boss could see my disapproval and declining engagement.

As my resentment for him and my situation grew, my self-esteem continued to erode. The constant anger inside me was poison. I felt trapped, weak, and small. I started acting out at business meetings and at random times in places like airports or grocery stores, snapping at people for trivial, perceived injustices. One early morning, dressed in my ridiculous pajamas, I screamed at the top of my lungs at the floor-installation guys who had knocked on our door. When I stopped for a breath, they told me they had arranged and confirmed the time with my wife, knowing that I was an early riser (sorry guys). I had gone from the cheerful teacher to a snarling junkyard dog.

At some point in the journey, I retreated from the good fight. I didn't think I was successful enough, smart enough, or man enough. I stopped caring in that deeper way, because caring was my liability. I felt ashamed for being so sensitive: too deep, too soft at the core. I thought caring made me lesser. My shame manifested in seething anger and separated me from my better self.

THE FALL

After one business meeting in some hotel in some city, I woke up mildly hungover and highly depressed. I hated my boss, my job, and the life I was accepting. I realize now that I was in a real depression and in a more fragile state than I knew. I felt so low that morning that I had thoughts about not living anymore. I reached into my bag for the phone to call my wife and instead found a drawing my daughter Abby had hidden before I left. The drawing was of a father and daughter holding hands. Below the stick figures it read, "Daddy, I don't like it when you go on trips. I miss you. Thank you for taking care of us. Such a good boy!"

I had missed too many goodnight kisses as well as my children's precious day-to-day lives. Unfortunately, when I *was home*, I was distracted and irritable—brooding and constantly checking e-mail.

I returned home Friday night of that week. Saturday morning, I sobbed on my knees in the mulch. As I was making coffee in our kitchen on Sunday morning, my wife walked over to me, took my face in her hands with tears in her eyes, and said, "You're so unhappy. This job, this lifestyle . . . *it's killing you.* You need to change your job, career, something. Now! Pursue your dreams. Get back to you, the happy, loving person who is kind and funny, who loves and cares about people. Fight back by being who you are. I love you so much. I will support you in whatever you do. Come back to me!"

I was a sad and fearful mess—but I was loved.

Permission. A flicker of light. Awake.

I resigned Monday morning.

My life. Time to own it.

> *"There is only one way to learn. It's through action."*
> —Paulo Coelho, *The Alchemist*

WHAT DID I DO NEXT?

I did what any guy in his midforties would do after resigning from his job: I sat around every day in my pajamas drinking coffee and binge-watching Netflix. No. That's not what I did. I was so tired of feeling bad and feeling less than I could be that I immediately went to work on myself. Like my wife said, I needed to *fight back* for who I am. I craved that for myself. I owed that to her and my children. Here is a list of the actions and practices I took up:

> **I WAS A SAD AND FEARFUL MESS—BUT I WAS LOVED. PERMISSION. A FLICKER OF LIGHT. AWAKE. I RESIGNED MONDAY MORNING. MY LIFE. TIME TO OWN IT.**

- I immediately went to see an amazing physician to get a physical and get every test imaginable—a full workup. Overall, I had always been active, so I was in decent health. But **I needed a routine of exercise and healthier eating.** (Less sugar—give it a try!)

- I got into a morning ritual of **prayer and meditation.** Nearly every top performer and guru does some form of

overcame me with a very simple truth attached to it. *I love people. I crave real connection with others. I deeply care.* I felt an indescribable joy and rush of energy. In that state, I thought about the happiest and most fulfilling moments of my life. True happiness and fulfillment had never been about my boss's approval, my title, my salary, or my status. My truest self is speaking to an audience, coaching people, building teams, training, and teaching with a caring heart.

For the first time, I fully understood that caring was my greatest strength. Caring (love) is the source of everything great I've ever done. Caring didn't make me weak. Caring made me strong. Caring gave me courage. *Caring was what made me an effective leader and trainer.* It was caring that led my teams to great success and why my team members stayed with me through so many changes. I had positive influence because people trusted my intentions. "You're different because you really care about us," so many have told me. During the sixteen of twenty years where I had direct reports, I had nearly 100 percent retention of those teams. I attribute any success I've had to a combination of surrounding myself with very talented people, caring about them, and helping them to be more successful.

There in the woods, something broke open in me. I was seeing that my truest and deepest self was love.

> **DURING THE SIXTEEN OF TWENTY YEARS WHERE I HAD DIRECT REPORTS, I HAD NEARLY 100 PERCENT RETENTION OF THOSE TEAMS. I ATTRIBUTE ANY SUCCESS I'VE HAD TO A COMBINATION OF SURROUNDING MYSELF WITH VERY TALENTED PEOPLE, CARING ABOUT THEM, AND HELPING THEM TO BE MORE SUCCESSFUL.**

I didn't feel ashamed anymore for caring, for loving people. I felt proud and energized. I wasn't afraid anymore to be me.

Later that day, I went to see Helen, my therapist. After patiently listening to me describe my epiphany, she said, "TJ, of course you are the way you are. God made you this way. [long pause for me to take it in] Every experience you've had has led you to this crucial point where you choose to be brave and live this way. Isn't it wonderful to be you? Who else would you want to be? [pause] Don't deny the world of your love and caring. Do something with it. Go out there and make a difference—we need you!"

WHY DID I WRITE THIS BOOK?

The shame of my vulnerability and my negative mind-set hurt every aspect of my life—I listened to the self-limiting lies in my head. I couldn't spend one more day of my precious life thinking and feeling that way. I decided to *live a path with heart*. I woke up and discovered that *my power is caring*.

More caring is what I'm fighting for. I want you to love yourself and your life, in spite of your suffering and challenges. There is a more caring way to bring your talents and spirit to the world. I want you to take up the sword because there isn't enough caring and kindness at home, at work, and in the world. Statistics about stress, divorce, addiction, workplace engagement, and trust are poor and haven't improved in years. Far too many of you are disillusioned and disengaged by uncaring cultures and a lack of role models. When we don't feel cared about, we stop caring.

Influence is the result of giving your time, attention, energy, and love. I want people in positions of influence at work and in their communities to look inside and ask if they are honoring the opportunity and responsibility of their roles and bringing their best to others or if they are small and self-serving. Caring is a weapon in a war on the greed and selfishness that damage leadership in organizations and communities. Leaders inspire by sharing. Others follow that example.

I'm not an academic, researcher, or guru. I'm an everyman with real-world experiences and scars. Sharing my stories, ideas, and experiences isn't about me—it's about shining a light into the darker spaces of other's lives and hearts. I had to write this book. I had to try because *I am you.*

BETTER DAYS AHEAD?

I ask all of my coaching clients if they believe their best days are ahead or behind them. In every instance, there is a long pause. Subconsciously, I think many people see their future as the grind, the rat race, or the toil of life with only the occasional interruption of joy sprinkled in.

I'm here to tell you that you *can* unlearn your limiting beliefs about yourself. You can awaken to your power to connect and influence others. Doing so will lead you to inspire the world around you.

You may wonder if you're enough, if you measure up to the external sources of approval's sense of who you're supposed to be. You try, but you can't quite suppress the big questions about who you are and whether your life has meaning.

Each of us is a broken fragment of glass. You don't fully understand the grand design, but through caring, you can shine light into the darker spaces of yourself and others. *The Caring Warrior* will inspire you to courageously choose to care, in your own unique way, for your family, your workplace, and your world. I want to create a next generation of Caring Warriors.

Your best days are ahead of you.

You are enough.

We need you.

A SIMPLE OVERVIEW OF CARING

Caring (as a verb): *feeling* affection or liking: *feeling* concern or interest. Caring is heartfelt.

Caring

- is our natural instinct;

- comes before intellectualizing the why, the what, and the how;

- lightens our sense of scarcity and fear;

- lifts us out of the clutches of our egos;

- drives us to take courageous action on the battlefields of life;

- creates, innovates, and pushes teams and companies to grow; and

- *caring inspires. Caring works.* **Caring is the answer.**

WHAT IS A CARING WARRIOR?

Several years ago, students in my leadership program gave me a samurai sword signifying that I had been like a samurai teacher—a sensei. Not being a martial artist, that gift was a very special recognition. In subsequent leadership courses, I brought in a licensed Sogobujutsu senior instructor and inspiring consultant, Dr. Michael Dunphy. He presented me with a print inscribed with the Japanese symbols (kanji) for *katsujinken*: "the life-giving sword." He said, "TJ, these symbols represent you. You fight for good. You care about people."

I didn't realize it then, but the Caring Warrior was conceived in me that day. Here is my creed, the creed of the Caring Warrior.

CARING WARRIOR'S CREED

I am a Caring Warrior because I am awake.

I *own* my life, I *give*, and I *share*.

I am at war with scarcity, ignorance, injustice, and selfishness.

I know that my strength comes from love.

I choose to care although it is often not easy or convenient.

I can be depended upon to be strong, trustworthy, and humane.

I confront those who bully and mistreat other human beings.

I embrace fear as necessary, but it will never keep me from my best self.

I do my best to demonstrate patience and kindness.

I am open and curious about learning and growth.

I always seek to become a better version of myself.

I recognize my gifts and talents and use them for good.

I am sensitive to the feelings of others and seek to be authentic.

I am grateful for what I have.

I always uphold integrity with myself and others.

I do not blame others for my disappointments.

I stand up for what is right.

I laugh, smile, and enjoy life.

THE STRUCTURE OF THE BOOK

Like all heroes, you must go on a journey. In *The Caring Warrior*, you will visit three battlegrounds on your journey. These are the beautiful battlegrounds of your life: the inner self, relationships with others, and the larger organization or world culture. On each battleground, you have a job to do: a call to action.

THE CARING WARRIOR'S JOURNEY

In Part One, **Awaken**—on the self-battleground—you are called to *awaken and own who you are.*

In Part Two, **Influence**—on the relationship battleground—you are called to *influence by giving.*

In Part Three, **Inspire**—on the culture battleground—you are called to *inspire by sharing.*

THE FIGHT OF THE CARING WARRIOR

AWAKEN. INFLUENCE. INSPIRE.

Awaken and *own* who you are.
Influence by *giving*.
Inspire your culture by *sharing*.

WHEN YOU BECOME A CARING WARRIOR, YOU WILL

- live a more purposeful and fulfilling life;

- love and embrace who you are with confidence;

- feel more engaged with and empowered to do your work;

- influence and inspire others around you;

- connect with others and develop better relationships;

- truly lead your companies, your teams, and your families; and

- experience more joy.

Dare to care.

Put on your armor. Grab your sword. Let's begin.

PART ONE

AWAKEN

BATTLEGROUND: THE SELF.

CALL TO ACTION: OWN WHO YOU ARE.

CHAPTER 1	CHAPTER 2	CHAPTER 3
FEEL	**AWAKEN**	**OWN**

"Say not, 'I have found the truth,' but rather, 'I have found a truth.' Say not, 'I have found the path of the soul.' Say rather, 'I have met the soul walking upon my path.' For the soul walks upon all paths. The soul walks not upon a line, neither does it grow like a reed. The soul unfolds itself, like a lotus of countless petals."

—Kahlil Gibran, *The Prophet*

CHAPTER 1

FEEL

"The warrior and the artist live by the same code of necessity, which dictates that the battle must be fought anew every day."

—Steven Pressfield, *The War of Art*

CARING LIVES BENEATH THE SURFACE

We nervously mingled, dreading the start of our weekend-long retreat. Growing up Catholic, Confirmation is one of the seven sacraments, the individual's initiation into the Church. A "search retreat" (a stage in our training) had brought together twenty teenagers from different schools on this late November weekend. "Bam-b-b-b-b-baam, b-b-b-b-baam," sounded the horns and music. Abruptly, adults in clown makeup streamed into the room and started slapping similar makeup on each of us participants. We looked at one another as if to say, "What have we gotten ourselves into?" For me, football season had just ended and Thanksgiving was the coming week, so this was not my ideal way to spend my entire weekend—doing "religious things."

We introduced ourselves to the group (torture for teenagers), and the head counselor explained that we all had the makeup on because we all wear masks in our everyday lives. The weekend was to be a search inside, underneath our masks—a step in the spiritual process. Still skeptical, we did a number of interactive group activities that actually turned out to be fun. Along with the others, I eventually opted to jump all the way in and make the most of the experience. What else could I do? Escape? Fully warmed up and energized, we broke off into small groups and were given a short questionnaire with three questions: What is the most important event in your life so far? What is the saddest/worst moment of your life? What are you happy about at this time in your life? *Wow*, I thought. Those were big questions for a fourteen-year-old.

I went first. The most important moment I shared was saving my brother's life in a near-fatal swimming incident. A great swimmer, he was also a risk-taker. He got stuck swimming through the ladder deep under our dock. I can still remember watching the dock and ladder shake as I tried to get him out. After a couple trips up to the surface and back down, I was able to push him out. After my high-intensity story, the group discussion was off and running. We continued around the circle.

I also shared that my worst moment was the day my father left our home before my parents' divorce. Hearing others' stories and sharing mine out loud for the first time gave me a buzz of closeness and connection. We were being real with each other—not like at school. A few others shared their worst moments, then I remember gulping and going numb when one member of my group told us that less than a year before, he had found his sister dead—a suicide.

Silence. Sadness. Empathy. Unprompted, digesting the gravity of the horrible experience our peer had gone through, we seven young girls and boys wrapped our arms around a relative stranger. Then and for many years after, I had no words to articulate the intimacy and impact of that moment. We had clown makeup on, but our masks had come off. We were "in it," facing the joys and the suffering that unite all human beings. Our inner goodness—our caring—connected us. The depth of that weekend demonstrated the power of caring in the inevitable battles of life. I knew then that I wanted to go deeper than the surface in my relationships. I wanted to know more about people and the stories of their lives.

OUR HERO STORIES

Each of us has a story. Our lives are hero stories: failure, redemption, pain, romance, and good-versus-evil triumph stories are all battles for the warrior. Every warrior faces battles of spirit, heart, and mind. Legendary story expert and writing teacher Robert McKee emphasizes that "story is a metaphor for life; stories are the creative conversion of life itself into a more powerful, clearer, more meaningful experience. They are the currency of human contact."[1] I believe that our story—our battles to be who we are and have a more meaningful and connected experience—is our training to be warriors. Our story is our call to grow, to lead, and to realize our potential.

---

1   Robert McKee, *Story: Style, Structure, Substance, and the Principles of Screenwriting* (HarperCollins: New York, 1997).

We follow the stories of our favorite mentors and role models, our favorite characters from books and movies, and our favorite sports heroes because we see ourselves in them. We root for them to overcome struggles, and we applaud their triumphs. These heroes inspire us with their leadership and courage because in them, we glimpse our own potential. As human beings, we connect to the story and the hero because we feel what they feel. Sure, I'd love to be Russell Crowe in the film *Gladiator*, but the point is that although I'm not actually wielding a sword in the arena with tigers and chariots and cheering Romans (man, that would be cool!), I connect to the themes of strength, honor, revenge, redemption, courage, love, and fear. The hero story of Maximus becomes mine because I am living my own version of those themes. We all are. We all face fear.

"Once there was a young warrior. Her teacher told her that she had to do battle with fear. She didn't want to do that. It seemed too aggressive; it was scary; it seemed unfriendly. But the teacher said she had to do it and gave her the instructions for the battle. The day arrived. The student warrior stood on one side, and fear stood on the other. The warrior was feeling very small, and fear was looking big and wrathful. They both had their weapons. The young warrior roused herself and went toward fear, prostrated three times, and asked, 'May I have permission to go into battle with you?' Fear said, 'Thank you for showing me so much respect that you ask permission.' Then the young warrior said, 'How can I defeat you?' Fear replied, 'My weapons are that I talk fast, and I get very close to your face. Then you get completely unnerved, and you do whatever I say. If you don't do what I tell

you, I have no power. You can listen to me, and you can have respect for me. You can even be convinced by me. But if you don't do what I say, I have no power.' In that way, the student warrior learned how to defeat fear."

—Pema Chödrön, *When Things Fall Apart: Heart Advice for Difficult Times*

A warrior's confrontation with fear is often thrust upon him or her. In *Crazy for the Storm*, Norman Ollestad tells us the harrowing story of a tragic plane crash in the San Gabriel Mountains of California when he was just eleven years old. He witnessed the death of his father and the pilot. Despite Ollestad's attempts to care for her, his father's girlfriend also passed away during their treacherous trek in a blizzard through the mountains after the crash. In the face of the tragedy, he faced unimaginable fear, summoning the warrior's inner spirit to survive. He never gave up. Ultimately, he made his way down the 8,600-foot mountain, where a family took him in and cared for him before reuniting him with his mother. I am humbled by his courage. Ollestad continued his heroic story, becoming an outstanding surfer, skier, and athlete as a young man. Later in life, he shared his incredible story in a memoir that went on to be a best seller in multiple categories. He continues to be a Caring Warrior as a family man, adventurer, and writer.

Our journeys start with separation from life as we know it. Life takes a turn for the worse. The status quo shifts out of balance. Call it "harsh reality." In stories, we call this the *inciting incident* that moves the hero into conflict and ultimately to action. Internally, when we are thrown into conflict, we have no choice but to respond. On the battleground of the self, these inner tests persist through life and can arise at any moment and in many different forms. No one escapes. We don't control the circumstances, only our response. Fear and uncertainty in challenging circumstances often thrust us into an emotional, mental, and spiritual fight-or-flight scenario. Of course, the fight here is symbol for having the courage to take the better course of action (honorable and positive), although that path scares us. The right, and often more difficult path, is the act of *taking up the sword* for the Caring Warrior. Not taking up the fight represents a choice we often see as the "safe" option—a choice we make because we don't believe we have what it takes. We don't believe that life is fair or that we will be rewarded for our courage. We believe we are limited. We place unwarranted limits on our potential. Our self-limiting beliefs are a form of surrender, and they cause us to suffer on the battleground because the war wages on whether or not we choose to participate. Our safe choice, or so we think, is actually the riskier response, because we suppress our warrior's spirit. Our mind-set—the way we think—is *scarcity*.

WHAT IS A SCARCITY MIND-SET?

"Most people are deeply scripted in what I call the Scarcity Mentality. They see life as having only so much, as though there were only one pie out there. And if someone were to get a big piece of the pie, it would mean less for everybody else.

The Scarcity Mentality is the zero-sum paradigm of life. People with a Scarcity Mentality have a very difficult time sharing recognition and credit, power or profit— even with those who help in the production. They also have a very hard time being genuinely happy for the success of other people."

—Stephen Covey, *The 7 Habits of Highly Effective People*

Our thinking leads to our behavior. Our behavior determines our outcomes.

SCARCITY THOUGHTS, BEHAVIORS, AND OUTCOMES

OUR THOUGHTS	OUR BEHAVIORS	OUTCOMES
scarcity thinking	selfish, clinging	chronic dissatisfaction
fear	small, reactive	unrealized potential
insecurity	approval seeking	inauthentic and fragile relationships
indifference	unaccountable	perpetual detachment; self-exile
distrusting	passivity, quitting	unfulfilled dreams; wasted gifts

When I was steeped in the scarcity mind-set, I was hurting. *People who feel hurt will hurt other people.* Consider bullies. They transfer their hurt and anger to others. Perhaps you have a tyrannical boss who is acting out his or her story, aware of it or not, and forcing you into the role of the victim. Bullying and hurtful behavior are rooted in insecurity.

Insecure people are never fully engaged, in part because they're too busy grasping for reassurance, making their performance inconsistent and transient. Insecure people can't trust others, because they don't trust themselves. Disconnection from their real (better) selves ironically makes them perpetually unfulfilled and selfish. Selfish preoccupation in their thoughts leads to habits of self-serving behavior. These people are willing to do almost anything to ensure their own short-term success, even at the expense and sacrifice of others, so their word is worthless, and their personal and work relationships are hollow or fractured.

At the root of this crippling insecurity is fear. When we live in fear, we're perpetually in a state of self-protection, insecurity, and separation. We view others as mere vehicles to help us feel better or as obstacles to our happiness. When the stakes appear to be our very survival, we ditch loyalty, decency, and simple humanity. But we can't escape the truth of personal cause and effect.

"You may fool the whole world down the pathway of years
And get pats on the back as you pass
But your final reward will be heartache and tears
If you've cheated the man in the glass."

—Peter Dale Wimbrow, Sr., *The Man in the Glass*

Prior to a large company meeting, a senior executive I will call Jack arranged to have a talented young associate named Ted join him on stage for a presentation. Of course, being asked to share the stage with one of the bigwigs was a great honor and career opportunity for him. The meeting began on a Monday; therefore, Jack demanded they meet for lunch on Sunday to review the content then rehearse together in the early afternoon. In order to be there for lunch and rehearsal, Ted, an employee based on the West Coast, would have to leave his family on a Saturday in order to be present for the Sunday plans. Late Sunday morning, Jack cancelled lunch but left the afternoon meeting vague saying that he would text Ted when he was ready. Midafternoon, Jack canceled the rehearsal, claiming to be too busy with work. Less than one hour later, on his way to the hotel gym, Ted spotted Jack in the lobby bar, acting like he'd been there drinking for quite some time.

In spite of his disappointment and lost time, Ted responded like a leader—a Caring Warrior. He went back to his hotel room and prepared to do the entire presentation himself. He believed in the higher purpose of the content and the meeting because others would benefit from the information.

The following morning on stage, unprepared and unrehearsed, the executive started to fumble through the presentation. Very gracefully, Ted took the slide clicker and delivered the content of the presentation beautifully. He saved the executive and the day. He responded with abundance over scarcity. I'm happy to report that Ted's career has blossomed, and thankfully, he has a large sphere of influence in his company.

Titles and roles are irrelevant. What matters is how you choose to be in the world. The "bigwig" was small. The young associate stood tall because of his abundance mind-set.

> **TITLES AND ROLES ARE IRRELEVANT. WHAT MATTERS IS HOW YOU CHOOSE TO BE IN THE WORLD.**

WHAT IS AN ABUNDANCE MIND-SET?

"The Abundance Mentality, on the other hand, flows out of a deep inner sense of personal worth and security. It is the paradigm that there is plenty out there and enough to spare for everybody. It results in sharing of prestige, of recognition, of profits, of decision making. It opens possibilities, options, alternatives, and creativity."

— Stephen Covey, *The 7 Habits of Highly Effective People*

ABUNDANCE THOUGHTS, BEHAVIORS, AND OUTCOMES

OUR THOUGHTS	OUR BEHAVIORS	OUTCOMES
abundance	sharing	satisfaction
positive	responsive	realized potential
courage	authenticity	reciprocal relationships
intention	accountability	dependability; self-assurance
trust	proactivity	creativity; opportunity

THE SIX MENTAL VIRTUES OF A CARING WARRIOR

1. **Abundance:** Abundance originates from gratitude for the gift of life. You're here. You are you. You are unique. There is no one like you before, now, or ever. You have the means and ability to love, lead, learn, and grow. You have a spirit, regardless of where you believe it came from. Thinking with abundance and gratitude is your rudder in rough water. Life won't be easy or fair sometimes, and it's not meant to be. I used to believe that I deserved more because I was basically good, and I got up each day to go to work. That was a flawed way to think, and it manifested in what I attracted

from life: negativity. The abundance mind-set is believing that there is enough love, opportunity, and success to go around.

2. **Positivity:** Positivity is less a philosophy and more a day-to-day way of being. I woke up to the reality that we can choose to be positive, and when we do, we can't help but feel better. Feeling happy and positive, we are more kind and generous to others. Positivity is a gift that continues to give. Being more positive is fun. I smile more at strangers and say hello. I sing with my kids. I thank God each morning for my wife and family. I respond more positively to life's challenges. I'm a flawed and imperfect man, but I'm getting better.

   I love Ellen DeGeneres. I love her for her positivity. She concludes every episode of *The Ellen DeGeneres Show* with, "Be kind to one another." My neighbor Charlie showed me kindness, not with words but with his presence at perhaps the lowest point of my life. It was a simple and positive act of kindness.

3. **Courage:** The greatest form of courage is to be who we are—to be aligned in our thinking, our actions, and our words. Author Brené Brown gave us her courageous TED talk (one of their most popular ever, with over twenty-five million views to date) in which she talks about vulnerability. Authenticity strikes a balance: "I'm vulnerable, and I'm real, but I also have a lot to bring,"[2] hitting that sweet spot between humility and courage.

---

2   Brené Brown, "The Power of Vulnerability," TED, https://www.ted.com/talks/brene_brown_on_vulnerability?language=en.

4. **Intention:** Intention is your purposeful, fighting spirit. Having purpose surpasses passion because purpose has teeth; it's gritty. Seth Godin's definition of grit is "the attitude of someone who realizes *he has the power to care* and is intent on doing something with it."[3] Enough said.

5. **Trust:** Trust is thick. Trust begins inside with self-trust: our integrity. Trust can't be bought, sold, or manipulated. It is hard earned and easily lost. My stepfather, Joe, taught me the Latin expression *facta non verba* (deeds not words). A Caring Warrior earns trust by what she does, not what she says.

6. **Justice:** Stu Weber describes in his book, *Tender Warrior: Every Man's Purpose, Every Woman's Dream, Every Child's Hope,* "The heart of the Warrior is a protective heart. The Warrior shields, defends, stands between, and guards . . . He invests himself in the energy of self-disciplined, aggressive action. By Warrior I do not mean one who loves war or draws sadistic pleasure from fighting or bloodshed. There is a difference between a warrior and a brute. A warrior is a protector . . . " Our sense of justice leads us to stand up for others whether we're helping an elderly person with his or her luggage on a plane or calling out rude and unkind behavior. Caring Warriors are guardians of goodness.

---

3   Seth Godin, *The Icarus Deception: How High Will You Fly?* (Penguin Group, 2012).

CHAPTER 2

AWAKEN

"I have learned to kiss the waves that throw me up against the rock of ages."

—Charles Haddon Spurgeon

Josh felt nervous before school and relieved when the day was over. He suffered bullying and unkind behavior. Josh hung a picture of his recently passed father in his locker, which a few students ripped down. Desperate to give him a chance at a new beginning, his mother moved him to a different school. At first, things weren't much better in the new school. He felt invisible, unworthy of connection. He described his life then as a puzzle: he was a piece, unsure of where to go and where he fit. Josh wanted to reach out to people and be seen. He wanted to matter and connect with people.

One day when Josh arrived at school, instead of walking through the door with his head down, summoning an uncommon warrior spirit, he decided to hold the door for the other students who were entering school. As they passed, he said, "Good morning. How are you? Hi, have a great day!" A few of the students said, "Hey, thanks." Most rolled their eyes and thought it was weird. Awkward as it may have felt, he was no longer invisible. He continued to hold the door every day after that. With each passing day, more and more school-mates said, "Hello." Some even began to smile and say, "Thanks."

Before long, Josh was part of the rhythm of the school day, like the morning announcements or the Pledge of Allegiance. The sarcasm and snickers faded away. Students began to look forward to his kind and friendly greeting. When students talked about Josh now, they spoke of him as nice, cool—a good guy. Everyone started calling him "the Doorman." There were smiles and pats on the back. The boy who once held his head down in fear walked taller through the hallway, receiving high fives and fist bumps.

I can imagine kids' voices saying, "Hey, Doorman!" He smiled and shined light into others' days. Josh Yandt was an example to others of courage and kindness in the face of fear. Everyone at school knew who he was. That spring something beautiful happened.

Josh "the Doorman" was crowned the prom king. They presented him with a crown and a decorated wooden door with hundreds of signatures and notes on it. He courageously transformed himself. He transformed an entire school.

Josh Yandt reflects, saying, "Opening doors gives hope that people care." Watch the video[4] and feel the movement of your Caring Warrior's spirit. One act of kindness can change the world.

WHAT DOES IT MEAN TO TRANSFORM?

To transform is to change in condition, nature, or character. What's the magic that transforms ordinary people like Josh into something greater than themselves? In a word, *disillusionment*. Disillusionment is breaking from previously held beliefs about ourselves and our circumstances. We have the power to unlearn our limited and separate view of ourselves when we realize that those beliefs and our way of functioning in the world is not working. All of life's ups and downs, twists and turns, carry with them an opportunity to change. It could be major failure, a breakup, or a change in your life that pitches you into struggle. The following are some examples:

- A role model disappoints you or hurts your self-esteem.

- You're cut from a team or replaced.

- You experience a devastating personal loss.

- You fail in a big way.

- You get fired or laid off.

- You get promoted to a position for which you're underprepared and don't know what you're doing.

- You abandon your own integrity.

- You are discriminated against, threatened, or treated unfairly.

---

4   WestJet, "Josh—opening doors and hearts," https://www.youtube.com/watch?v=PlHtuKc3Gjg.

- Your feelings or pride are deeply hurt.

Confronting life-altering challenges isn't something most people do voluntarily. Shakespeare put it succinctly: "Some are born great, some achieve greatness, and some have greatness thrust upon 'em."[5] Life thrusts a conflict upon us, disrupting our lives and creating a new awareness and breakthrough opportunity. This breakthrough occurs when we clearly see the gap between where and what we are and where and what we want to be. As warrior heroes, the gap between who we are and who we want to be is found in the battle with ourselves. We can either look straight at ourselves (our life, who we are), or we can look away.

WHAT IF WE LOOK AWAY?

If in our discomfort and fear, we choose to listen to those mind monsters (negative self-talk) and look away, we believe that something or someone outside ourselves will make us feel better.

I'll feel better about myself and my life when I have my boss's approval. Get more recognition. Win an award. Get a new job title or promotion. Complete this project. Change jobs. Have more money. Achieve fame. Find a romantic partner. Take a vacation. Look better. Have a flat stomach. Buy something for myself. Get Mom or Dad's approval. When I beat this or that guy.

When we hand over the controls to someone else or hitch our self-esteem to some empty goal we've carved out as a yardstick for

---

5   William Shakespeare, *Twelfth Night*, 2.5.

ourselves, we surrender our power to change our life. When we operate from a place of fear, we are at the mercy of the changing winds of life's ups and downs, of outside forces. We let them blow us this way and that, remaining perpetually lost and small. We can blame all those outer forces for our unhappiness and dissatisfaction. I blamed my bad bosses, I blamed *them* and *they*—you know, "the bad guys." It was easier to put my anger on others than it was to break through my own spiritual laziness.

The fact is, we either choose to hand our life over to outside approval and acceptance, or we wake up and take ownership of that life. Owning our life is the greatest act of love we can give ourselves. Caring Warriors choose love over fear.

> **OWNING OUR LIFE IS THE GREATEST ACT OF LOVE WE CAN GIVE OURSELVES. CARING WARRIORS CHOOSE LOVE OVER FEAR.**

"In any given moment, we are either aligned mentally and emotionally with fear or with love."

—Joey Klein, *The Inner Matrix*

I wear a red rubber band on my wrist. I snap it against my wrist if I begin to get fearful or to listen to negative self-talk, thinking that I'm not enough. My mentor, Steve Cesari, calls this the *junk in your trunk*. The junk are just thoughts, most of them lies that we tell ourselves. We can willingly experience and accept our feelings and thoughts, but they do not have the last word about who we are and how we behave. We choose.

In *The Tao of Abundance*, Laurence G. Boldt writes, "It is not necessary for you to earn one more dollar, get a better job, buy a new home or car, or go back to school. All that is required is that you become *aware* of the inner process through which you create an experience of lack and struggle in your life and refrain from doing it. Feelings of abundance and gratitude are natural to the human being; they do not need to be added or put on." *Everything we need is within us.* We only need to awaken to it.

I coach individuals and teams. My greatest challenge is breaking through the barriers of fear and self-denial: fear of self-awareness and fear of taking responsibility. Fear has the potential to protect us from danger, stimulating our "gut reactions" or intuition about unsafe circumstances, but fear serves us better from the backseat, not the driver's seat. We transform our lives by taking back the wheel, by looking at who we are and who we want to be. We change where we are to where we want to be.

WE CAN TRANSFORM. WE CAN SEE OUR GREATNESS. WE CAN SERVE.

We can transform. We can see our greatness. We can serve.

Abraham Lincoln, one of our greatest leaders, lived out a nearly mythological hero story, rising from a one-room cabin to the White House. Largely self-taught, he failed at a number of ventures in his early years. His beginnings were humble to say the least, yet he knew he had something within to share. He possessed the potential for greatness. In spite of his challenges and losses, Lincoln remained steadfast and never caved in to the unfairness of life. He suffered from depression during stages of his life, yet he was known for his optimism, uncompromising honesty, and kindness.

During his presidency, he spent much of his time visiting wounded soldiers and attending the funerals of the fallen. In *Lincoln on Leadership*, Donald T. Phillips writes, "This striking visible display of compassion and caring on the part of the president inspired trust, loyalty, and admiration not just from the soldiers but also from his subordinates." Lincoln elegantly held all the complexities of being human in one strong, tender, and committed heart. He changed history with his service, his intelligence, and his leadership, all of which grew from his caring spirit. He transformed his circumstances and transformed the course of history by picking up his sword. Lincoln owned his life and fought for his possibilities, which influenced and inspired so many others.

WHAT WE SEE VERSUS WHAT WE WANT TO BE

SCARCITY MINDED		ABUNDANCE MINDED
negative		positive
reactive		proactive
selfish	CHANGE	generous
arrogant		humble
blaming		accountable
micromanaging		empowering
tyrannical		coaching
defeating		inspiring

Transformation (change)—becoming a warrior, the "picking up of the sword" is a major theme in history and fiction. Famous warrior cultures in history such as the Spartans or samurai are known to have endured grueling initiation and training for the honor of protecting and caring for their lords and people. Each warrior culture identifies with a code. Sir Lancelot and the Knights of the Round Table had a code of chivalry—a moral system whereby the knights were expected to show bravery, courtesy, honor, gallantry, and heart.

We know the challenge of becoming heroic is the more difficult path. And so, we root for fictional characters on their journeys. The character Rey takes up her lightsaber in *Star Wars: The Force Awakens*. King Arthur accepts Excalibur from the Lady of the Lake. Dorothy in *The Wizard of Oz* claims the witch's broom. The hero has moved further away from her fear and ego to her real self: the godlike part of her. She accepts more responsibility in the world. A hero wins his or her title by risking individual life for the larger, collective life.

> **A HERO WINS HIS OR HER TITLE BY RISKING INDIVIDUAL LIFE FOR THE LARGER, COLLECTIVE LIFE.**

One of my favorite literary characters is David Copperfield. He epitomizes the sensitive hero (Caring Warrior). He experiences pain and disappointments heaped upon him by heartless scoundrels throughout Dickens's novel, yet rather than become negative and bitter, he looks straight at his life, faces the outside forces, and chooses to be an honorable man.

> *"My meaning simply is, that whatever I have tried to do in life, I have tried with all my heart to do well; that whatever I have devoted myself to, I have devoted myself to completely; that in great aims and in small, I have always been thoroughly in earnest."*
>
> —Charles Dickens, *David Copperfield*

In Disney's *The Lion King*, Simba, suppressing guilt for his father's death and denying his destiny to be king, devotes himself to the mantra, "Hakuna matata," a Swahili phrase that means "no worries." He becomes the hero of the story when he looks in the pond and sees his future as king of the pride. His tribe (pride) needs him. He cares enough to take ownership of his life. He courageously rediscovers his fighting spirit and transforms into warrior-king.

There's no easy path to get where you're going; leading is what the hero does *after* his or her ordeal. It's not until that hard-won self-knowledge is gained that a more authentic life can unfold. You earn the right to self-esteem when you go to work on yourself. Owning who you are allows you to reach your potential as a leader, influencer, and inspiration to others. A quote attributed to Ernest Hemingway says it well: "There is no nobility in being better than somebody else. The nobility is in being a better version of yourself."

> **TRANSFORMING TAKES A CARING WARRIOR'S COURAGE. DARE TO CARE.**

Transforming takes a Caring Warrior's courage. Dare to care.

CHAPTER 3

OWN

"The greatest crime we commit against ourselves is not that we may deny or disown our shortcomings, but that we deny and disown our greatness—because it frightens us."

—Nathaniel Branden, *The Six Pillars of Self-Esteem*

Earlier in my career, I mentored Ashley, a smart and highly driven new manager. Prior to her promotion, she had been a high performer and leader among her peers. She was held up as an exemplary model for behaviors and performance metrics. Then she became "the boss," and suddenly, she was hell on wheels.

What went wrong? The notion of working through others was very hard for her to acclimate to. After all, she had always been in control of her own destiny. She worked hard, was very competent in her role, and rarely needed to ask for help. Now she had ten people reporting to her, many of whom were in their first year on the job and in the industry. I was called upon to coach her because she had never reported to me, so I could be a more objective guide into the role. Things were already going poorly with her and her team. There had been rumblings that the team was not happy. The feedback was not lost on her, and she was defensive about it. She was doing her own rumbling with her new management colleagues and telling them how incompetent and lazy some team members were. It was a bad situation.

During our first couple of conversations, she vented her frustrations. I heard a lot of "I think," "I feel," "I want," "I believe," and "they should." Then it progressed to "I'm tired," "I work harder and longer than I ever have," and "I hate this. I know how to do the job. I can just tell them what they need to do."

Look at what I've shared above—can you spot the common thread? It's all *I*—all about her. She thought the job was about her.

I was empathetic because she was very early in her career, she'd never managed people before, and she hadn't been developed for the role. Moving her into management was simply viewed as the next step—bigger title, more money, and theoretically more influence. But she was failing. I was asked to be her mentor after the situation went bad.

I acknowledged, "Leading others is difficult. It wasn't what I expected either. I struggled, and I brought all my insecurities and baggage into the job. It's hard for a successful person like you to feel like you're failing. Are you committed to turning things around?"

"Of course. Yes!"

"Awesome. Can I shoot you straight and then ask you some questions?"

She nodded. "Please! I need to figure this out, quit, or worse, get fired. I need to show everyone that I can do the job and get results. I need to prove myself. I don't want to fail. I can't!"

"You will figure this out, Ashley. First, you have to ask yourself why you're doing the job. I think you'll find that leading people isn't about you. It starts with self-awareness, but ultimately it's about the team and the unique people on that team. You have to make a commitment to work with and through others and to put them first. Their success will ultimately be your success, but not until you back off on what you want and why you want it and find out what's on *their* minds. You have to find out what matters to them. You can only realize *your* full potential if you put your emotional effort and mental energy into *them*. Did you know any of your people before you became their manager?"

"I knew about half of them as acquaintances. The others are new to me. Of course, I didn't hire any of them. It's not my fault if someone else hired the wrong people."

"Either way, Ashley, they need you, and you need them. Have you sat down with each of them, one-on-one, to break the ice and share a little about yourself and, more importantly, learn about them? There is no more important investment you can make than your time, energy, and face-to-face attention." Outside of reviewing sales performance and targeting (mostly by phone), she hadn't. And she didn't have any idea what that might look like, so I offered her some ideas to start over and change her approach. I suggested that she immediately adjust her calendar to prioritize one-on-one, face-to-face meetings with her direct reports. I told her to turn off her phone.

I said, "Get to know them as people. Ask about their backgrounds: Where are they from? How did they get here? Do they have families? Significant others? What gets each of them out of bed every morning to go to work (which they do, hopefully)? What's working for them? What isn't? Ask one or two things you can do right away to help. Find out what they respond to best with a manager or supervisor. Respect their expectations of you, and they will then respect the expectations you have of them. Listening to their expectations first will give you the insights to state and adjust the delivery of your expectations."

It sounds so simple, but this is how we make the human connection and lay the foundation for a trusting relationship. Ashley was quiet but listening. I said, "Ashley, you have to connect with them before you can lead them. They will respect and appreciate that you've taken the time to learn about them."

> ## YOU MUST CONNECT WITH OTHERS BEFORE YOU CAN LEAD THEM.

Her team wanted to know that they were seen as individuals, with lives and purpose beyond the office. They wanted to know that she cared enough to ask and that she was as committed to them as she expected them to be to her.

I finished by saying, "Look, we all respect you and what you've accomplished. There's no question in my mind that you'll have a top-producing team, but not if they don't trust you and not if they don't think you care. Your reputation only gets you in the door. How you treat them is what determines how successful you will be together. When you know what motivates and inspires each of them, you will have a much better chance of coaching and developing them to higher performance. Look, Ashley, we want you to do well, but you won't, and they won't, without that foundation of trust, because they will only accept your expertise and coaching when trust is established. You have to decide if you care about them—their success and their development. Otherwise, you can't influence and lead them."

At this point, she broke down. She admitted, "I am failing. I'm failing them *and* the company. I've just never done this before. But I need to start over. Press reset. I have to change how I'm going about this. I want them to trust me. We'll all be miserable if they don't trust me. I have been on teams where only a couple people stood out, and I have been on teams when everyone got along and we all won. That was much more fun. This team has potential to be great. What can I do differently?"

Eureka! She got it. She had been terrified to fail. She was leading from fear. She was unhappy, and therefore, she made her team unhappy. After this realization, a very different type of leader emerged—one who knew that she had to work on herself. She asked me for book recommendations. She attended several leadership courses. I continued to be her mentor, and we spoke at least once per week. She grew because she chose to transform. Her team(s) went on to do very well, and she eventually was promoted into greater roles of responsibility. All I did was hold up the mirror. She took ownership, which ultimately made her a much better leader.

OWN YOUR LIFE FIRST IN ORDER TO HELP OTHERS

When flying, in the event of an emergency, the flight attendant instructs passengers to first put

> CARING WARRIORS CANNOT FIGHT, PROTECT, DEFEND, AND PERFORM THEIR DUTIES UNLESS THEY HAVE TAKEN RESPONSIBILITY AND CHOOSE TO BE THEIR *CARING* BEST.

the oxygen mask on themselves in order to help others. And so it is with warriors. They cannot fight, protect, defend, and perform their duties unless they have taken responsibility and choose to be their *caring* best.

How do you transform and take ownership of your better self—your Warrior spirit?

You have power to change and grow when you awaken and say to yourself, *I own it!*

I. O.W.N. I.T.

I: IDENTITY

There's a very revealing teaching activity in which you pair two people and give them three to five minutes to draw one another. When adults share their drawings, they inevitably apologize—"Wow. This looks so ridiculous. I'm so sorry." However, children who do the activity are proud of what they drew. Children believe they are great artists. We are not born cynical and negative. From the start, kids believe in themselves and in their heroic potential. Children say, "I want to be a superhero. I want to go to the moon. I want to be a famous singer." Anything is possible. There are no limits. Our view of ourselves gets tamped down as we grow up.

HOW WE VIEW OURSELVES IS OUR IDENTITY.

How we view ourselves is our identity. Underneath the influence and input we take from the outside world, there is a deeper truth about who we are. Many call it the *soul*. I believe our soul is the precious life force where all love and possibility exists. Our self-esteem nurtures and protects that precious soul.

The late Dr. Nathaniel Branden, foremost thinker and writer on self-esteem, teaches us that self-esteem is the result of possessing the heroic courage to claim who we are and then to act upon it. In other words, self-esteem—the realization of our identity—is not just a birthright but a *practice*.

Branden's *Six Pillars of Self-Esteem:*

- The Practice of Living Consciously: living with self-awareness and mindfulness

- The Practice of Self-Acceptance: being who you are

- The Practice of Self-Responsibility: acknowledging your thoughts, words, and actions as your own

- The Practice of Self-Assertiveness: taking action based on your intuition and determination

- The Practice of Living Purposefully: realizing your identity is your purpose, your call in life

- The Practice of Personal Integrity: holding yourself to a standard of behavior aligned with your values

We will explore the components and realization of your identity in the journal exercises at the end of this section. For now, I will leave you with Dr. Branden's rhetorical question: "But does anything take more courage—is anything more challenging and sometimes frightening—than to live by our own mind, judgment, and values? Is not self-esteem a summons to the hero within us?"[6]

---

6   Nathaniel Branden, *The Six Pillars of Self-Esteem* (New York: Bantam Books, 1994).

O: OPENNESS

A key component of owning our lives is opening ourselves to others. Bruce Lee said, "We have to empty the cup in order to fill it." When we open ourselves, we take self-responsibility for our learning and growth, for our potential. Caring Warriors care about becoming better versions of themselves. A Caring Warrior's openness is demonstrated in the following ways:

- He is curious and receptive to his own creativity and new ideas.

- She pays attention to her intuition and sees value in it.

- He engages in honest and open communication, giving and receiving feedback.

- She learns from failure and mistakes in the spirit of progress.

- He welcomes new input and interactions as an opportunity to grow.

W: WILL

Carol Dweck teaches us in her book *Mindset*, "This growth mindset is based on the belief that your basic qualities are things you can cultivate through your efforts." Our potential for achievement and fulfillment is not predetermined or fixed. The life we live is determined by how we see ourselves and our willingness to grow, take action, and improve.

GARRETT'S STORY

Garrett's destiny hung on the outcome of a coin toss. If the coin landed "heads," he made the freshmen crew (rowing) team. If it landed "tails," he would be cut. The last spot on the roster came down to Garrett and another freshman. Heads!

Of course, Garrett Miller never knew this until many years later. When I met him, I was a new teacher at the very special La Salle College High School in the Philadelphia suburbs. I was one of the football coaches in the fall. In the spring, the head coach of the varsity crew team, Pete Sigmund, invited me to help out. I had heard of rowing but knew nothing about the sport, so my job was to drive the rowers in a shuttle bus to and from the river and to keep Pete company while he coached the team and drove the skiff. I asked Pete to teach me and to tell me about his very best rowers.

———————

After making the rowing team, Garrett and his team-mates struggled to learn the rowing technique and to get in shape. One day, training on land, the team did uphill wind sprints. People were throwing up, and many quit. At the time, Garrett was five foot four and weighed two hundred pounds. He wasn't necessarily unathletic, but he was badly out of shape. In the summer of that year, Garrett decided he was "going to be someone special." He didn't want to be the last guy picked ever again. So he went to work.

Garrett spent that summer—between freshmen and sophomore year—the same way he spent all his summers: cleaning industrial heaters with a hardworking man, Pasquale "Pat" Staffeiri. The day started early and ended in the late afternoon. From there, Garrett went to the local gym/health club every day. By Christmas, he'd lost some weight and felt better, and he asked his parents for one present: an indoor rowing machine, or "erg." He rowed every day, sometimes twice; once before work and once when he got home from the gym.

When I met Garrett, he was the senior captain of the La Salle rowing team. After I asked Pete to tell me about his best rowers, he said, "Garrett Miller is a rowing stud. He's like a freak of nature. I've never had a rower work harder to transform himself."

As a senior in high school, Garrett was six foot four and weighed a buff 215 pounds. He had naturally grown taller, but through discipline and consistent hard work, he transformed his body. He fell in love with the sport. He told me, "Something just clicked. I kicked it into high gear. I didn't want to be invisible." He was certainly noticed. He earned a scholarship to the Ivy League University of Pennsylvania to row.

That was the last I knew of Garrett for several years because I changed careers, moved, and started a family. In 2003, I met Garrett's mother and aunt at a random business luncheon. We quickly made the connection. I choked back tears when they informed me that he had gone on to participate and win (with his eight-man crew) three world championships in a row. In 2000, Garrett rowed in the Olympics. In 2014, Garrett was inducted into the Rowing Hall of Fame.

After reconnecting years later, Garrett told me about his induction event and how the honor made him look back on the journey that began when he barely made the freshman team. He talked about the many coaches and teammates who inspired him. He told me that he felt humbled by competing with and against the best in the world. He shared the importance of hard work and commitment. I asked him, "Garrett, what was the key to your success?"

He responded, "I decided. I was going to outwork and outlast." While at Penn, Garret woke at 4:00 a.m. and drove from Philadelphia to Princeton, New Jersey, to row with some of best rowers in the country. After the sunrise workout, he drove back for a full day of classes, hit the gym, and attended Penn's crew practice. He said, "I wanted to not only raise my own performance but lift everyone around me to a higher level." He went on, "There were moments out there on the water, pulling off the line, continuously recommitting moment to moment, where we were floating on air—everything beautifully in sync. Spiritual. I'm really grateful for those experiences."

I responded, "You made them happen, Garrett."

If we surrender our will in the face of uncertainty, fear, or disappointment, we risk not developing to our full potential. What about you? How do you begin?

The first step is *deciding*. This is much easier said than done. I believe we have a natural instinct to care about the lives we live—to realize our potential. As I've said before, realization is never the result of passivity. Realization of who we are requires fierce caring and determination.

We keep our *will* by making progress. Take small actions to move forward. Our doubts and fears overwhelm us because we believe where we want to be is too far a journey, and there's no guarantee we will achieve what we

WE CREATE A FALSE REALITY WHEN WE LISTEN TO THE VOICES OF DOUBT.

desire. We imagine all the potential setbacks and dangers of the road ahead and often fail to take any small steps forward. We create a false reality when we listen to the voices of doubt. Break down your intentions (your goals, desires, or changes) into smaller steps. Will yourself to just take one step, then the next.

Garrett Miller chose personal excellence. He made himself an amazing athlete because he took ownership of his life and his future. His progress to that goal was a steady climb of small individual moment-to-moment recommitments, as he calls them. The countless predawn trips to the river, erg workouts in his basement, nutrition, rest, and hours in the gym—he climbed his way up step-by-step, believing enough to put one foot in front of the other. Summon your will, your *inner warrior*, to begin your climb.

N: NOW

Jewish sage scholar Rabbi Hillel said, "If I am not for myself, then who will be for me? And if I am only for myself, then what am I? And if not now, when?"[7] Do it now! There is no better time than now to be, to own who you are. We are constantly angry and resentful about the past and projecting fear into the future. We need to be in the present moment. What else do we have but *now*? Reflect on your current situation in order to change. Take an inventory like I did. Wake up and take action now. Find your soul while walking.

I: INTEGRITY

Enmeshed in each moment of our lives is our integrity—what we stand for. Fundamental to owning our lives as Caring Warriors is our personal ethos, or code of ethics. At times, we allow ourselves to be

---

7   "Quotes on Judaism & Israel: Rabbi Hillel," http://www.jewishvirtuallibrary.org/jsource/Quote/hillel.html.

at the mercy of the circumstances of the day, and because life is challenging, we react based on emotion and perception. Our integrity represents an opportunity to hold more firmly and consistently.

Knowing what we stand for lessens the frequency of ineffective actions and words. Our integrity determines our relationships with others and ourselves because breaches of integrity are withdrawals from the self-esteem bank account. Speaking and acting in alignment with integrity, even when we have to stand alone, are deposits in that bank account. A caring warrior holds inner and outer integrity.

Many authority figures say the right words but don't behave consistently with those words. Mark McDade is a man who stands up to do the right thing for his people. He was CEO of a biotech company I worked for some years back. During the early days of a forthcoming acquisition and downsizing, Mark knew that many people would lose jobs and feel a great amount of stress. The day of the announcement, he traveled across the country to Boston, where his leadership team was meeting, to show each of us his support in person. Mark could have called a teleconference or sent a group e-mail, as is so often done. He cared enough to show up. That evening, he made a point of speaking one-on-one with every individual. Mark's personal integrity trumped whatever business issues competed for his time and attention.

CARE ENOUGH TO SHOW UP.

T: TRUTH

"The truth needs no defense."

—Eckhart Tolle, *A New Earth*

Reflecting back on his life in his final days, my father told me, "The truth will set you free." These words from my dad affected me very much because they showed me that by the time you reach the end of your life, you want to be free of any lies or self-delusions. Our warrior's journey to become who we are meant to be—our most powerful and caring self—requires our commitment to truth, to unfiltered honesty with ourselves and others. Trust of self, trust of others, and trustworthiness begin with uncompromising truth.

For a Caring Warrior, truth can get muddy in the chaos of life. We will struggle to trust our own judgment. We will be tempted to bend memory to validate our behavior and justify our actions. We may accept small and large untruths from others around us. We might manipulate or omit facts to enhance our circumstance or protect ourselves. We can become numb to the insincerity and dishonesty we see in those we expect to lead us. We may lower our expectations of the people we follow, eroding our personal boundaries that separate right from wrong. Fighting off this chaos and temptation, a Caring Warrior is a guardian of truth.

We only get better through ongoing self-evaluation and by making a personal promise that we will hold ourselves accountable for improvement. Truth, and our dedication to it, is a daily battle for the Caring Warrior—diet, exercise, spiritual prayer, gratitude, goal setting, journaling, emotional control, and self-development. These disciplines keep us closer to truth.

Devotion to truth is the foundation of the Caring Warrior's self-mastery.

SUMMARY

- Choose to become a Caring Warrior.

- Stop and take an inventory of your life.

- Look straight into the mirror and see past your fear.

- Love who you are: the person God made you to be.

- Take up the sword. Change. Transform. Care.

- Realize your potential.

- Own your life.

- Love.

- Repeat.

"Let go with your heart. Let go with your head. Feel it now."

—David Gray, "Babylon"

EXERCISES

"Outstanding leaders take time to reflect. Their success depends on the ability to access their unique perspective and bring it to their decisions and sense-making every day," writes Nancy J. Adler in her January 16th, 2016, *Harvard Business Review* article.

The pen is one of the Caring Warrior's weapons. Many of our leaders, artists, and thinkers have made journaling a daily practice, including Ben Franklin, Winston Churchill, Sacagawea, Anne Frank, Ernest Hemingway, and Mozart.

GRAB YOUR PEN. TAKE YOUR RIGHTFUL PLACE AMONG THE GREATS.

1. On a scale of one to ten, what is your level of happiness and fulfillment? Explain.

2. What matters most to you? Who and what do you value? (Examples: spouse/significant other, work performance, work relationships, finances, home, family, health, spirituality/faith, education, etc.)

3. Based on what matters most to you, where are the gaps in your level of fulfillment?

4. What are your most persistent negative thoughts? What percentage of your negative thinking is based on truth?

5. Discuss your experience of negative or scarcity thinking and the "right-now" present moment. Be sure to consider how much of your thinking is originating from past upsets or future worries.

6. How are your negative thoughts affecting your level of happiness and fulfillment?

7. List each negative thought or narrative and write out the exact opposite. Example: I will always be overweight and unattractive. Opposite: I am lean, attractive, and I feel great about my body. Write it. Then say it. Say it. Say it.

8. What are you most grateful for?

9. What do you do to honor those blessings in your life? What can you do to nurture those blessings and appreciate them?

10. What does a better version of yourself feel like? What does it look like?

11. What can you do to *own* your life and the path you want to walk?

SENTENCE COMPLETION

(These are only suggestions/starters. Don't censor yourself. Write whatever comes to mind. This is for you alone.)

I am . . .

I spend my time and energy . . .

I believe . . .

I care about . . .

I will . . .

PGA: PRIORITIES, GOALS, ACTIONS

"You will never be able to escape from your heart. So it's better to listen to what it has to say."

—Paulo Coelho, *The Alchemist*

Name:

Date:

PRIORITIES • GOALS • ACTIONS

Personal Mission Statement:

What is your vision? Why do you do what you do?
List a statement or quote that drives you.

Priorities:

Guiding principles—what matters most to you? Ex: family, health, and chruch/spirituality, career, financial, charity, integrity...

PGA: PRIORITIES, GOALS, ACTIONS

PRIORITIES • GOALS • ACTIONS

Goals:

What do you want to accomplish based on your priorities? WHY is this goal important to you? How will you know you've accomplished it? When will you achieve this goal? Write your goal in the affirmative: "I am..."

Goal 1:

Goal 2:

Goal 3:

PGA: PRIORITIES, GOALS, ACTIONS

PRIORITIES • GOALS • ACTIONS

Actions:

What specific actions will you take daily/weekly to achieve those goals? What are you committed to doing consistently?

Goal 1:

Actions:

Goal 2:

Actions:

Goal 3:

Actions:

RESOURCES

BOOKS/ARTICLES

- *It Was On Fire When I Lay Down On It*, Robert Fulghum

- *The Alchemist*, Paolo Coelho

- *The Prophet*, Kahlil Gibran

- *A Path with Heart*, Jack Kornfield

- *The Art of War*, Steven Pressfield

- *STORY: Style, Structure, Substance, and the Principles of Screenwriting*, Robert McKee

- *When Things Fall Apart: Heart Advice for Difficult Times*, Pema Chödrön

- *Crazy for the Storm*, Norman Ollestad

- *The 7 Habits of Highly Effective People*, Steven Covey

- *The Icarus Deception*, Seth Godin

- *Tender Warrior; Every Man's Purpose, Every Woman's Dream, Every Child's Hope*, Stu Weber

- *Twelfth Night*, William Shakespeare

- *The Inner Matrix*, Joey Klein

- *The Tao of Abundance*, Laurence G. Boldt

- *Lincoln on Leadership*, Donald T. Phillips

- *David Copperfield*, Charles Dickens

- *Mindset*, Carol Dweck

- *A New Earth*, Eckart Tolle

- *The Six Pillars of Self-Esteem*, Nathaniel Branden

- "Want to be an Outstanding Leader? Keep a Journal," Nancy J. Adler, *Harvard Business Review*, January 2016, https://hbr.org/2016/01/want-to-be-an-outstanding-leader-keep-a-journal.

QUOTES/POEMS/SONGS/VIDEOS/FILMS

- "The Man in the Glass," Peter Dale Winbrow (poem)

- "Babylon," David Gray (song)

- *Gladiator*

- *Star Wars: The Force Awakens*

- *The Wizard of Oz*

- *Good Will Hunting*

- *The Lion King*

- Brené Brown, "The Power of Vulnerability," TedTalk, https://www.ted.com/talks/brene_brown_on_vulnerability?language=en.

- Josh Yandt, "The Doorman," https://www.youtube.com/watch?v=PIHtuKc3Gjg.

PART TWO

INFLUENCE

BATTLEGROUND: RELATIONSHIPS.

CALL TO ACTION: INFLUENCE BY GIVING.

CHAPTER 4	CHAPTER 5	CHAPTER 6
CONNECT	**GIVE**	**INFLUENCE**

"Not only do self-love and love of others go hand in hand but ultimately they are indistinguishable."

—M. Scott Peck, *The Road Less Traveled: A New Psychology of Love, Traditional Values, and Spiritual Growth*

CHAPTER 4

CONNECT

*"Seeking the very best in ourselves means actively caring
for the welfare of other human beings."*

—*The Art of Living: The Classical Manual on Virtue, Happiness, and Effectiveness* by Epictetus and Sharon Lebell

As part of a twelve-month management-development program, I once took a group of ten people on a three-day leadership retreat. They had been identified as high-potential future leaders. Most of them knew one another, but very few were friends. In fact, you could feel the competitive tension in the room on the first day.

During one particular simulation, I gave them a task to perform with a three-minute time limit. I said, "In order to win, you must finish the task with no mistakes, in under three minutes. You will have three tries." Not surprisingly, given the composition of the group and the qualities for which they were selected, the ten of them assumed that it was a competition among the group, not a group problem for them to solve together against the clock. With that mind-set, individuals made attempts that used up three attempts very quickly. Their three attempts all failed. Naturally, they were frustrated and not happy with me. They were used to winning. In the roughly fifteen minutes from the time I gave them the task until the third failed attempt, things had gone downhill fast. There were disagreements, sarcasm, blaming, and interruptions.

Mike said, "Oh TJ, I get it. The point is to fail. You made it impossible."

"No, not true," I replied.

Denise said, "Okay, what time is lunch?" It was 10:00 a.m.

I knew this would be the reaction. They were falling right into the learning trap I'd set. Situations like this are a real microcosm of what can happen when people are relatively new to each other and they're given a task or a challenge. People understandably want to prove themselves. They sort of a pounce on the ball as if it's a fumble or something, thinking, *I need to get it before everyone else does.*

AM I TRYING TO LOOK GOOD OR DO GOOD?

After some very rich discussion and conversation, Linda, one of the quieter participants, spoke up thoughtfully: "We didn't work together, because we were too worried about winning for ourselves. Everyone spoke over one another. Some of us never had an opportunity to say anything. We were afraid of looking bad." She called it; they were stymied by fear and their unwillingness to listen, and they all lost. By not considering the group and not allowing for individual input serving the greater good, everyone failed. Everyone was disappointed.

I asked each of the participants to write down what they were thinking and feeling under time pressure to perform. We discussed how the desire to "get it done" and to win had blocked a winning solution for the group. I pointed out that I never said it was an individual competition. I only told them the objective, the time limit, and what it meant to win. I explained that the only possible way to solve the simulation problem was to do it together, and they had overlooked that possibility three times. Tom spoke up and joked with the group, "We're here for *leadership* training! Guess we forgot?"

I laughed along with them and said, "Leaders look through a different lens. They face every challenge looking for ways to lift up everyone, not just themselves. Lighten up! It's just an exercise—I knew it would get you all thinking and talking." Wanting to win is awesome, but as leaders, the objective is to win without it being at the expense of others. Then, I asked them if they wanted to try it again: *"Yes!"* I heard a few pound the table with conviction as they got up. I gave them seven minutes to plan a strategy. Then they took another crack at it.

In the many times I've done similar exercises, a successful completion of the simulation is meant to take about twenty-five to thirty seconds with practice and improvement on each of the three attempts. This group completed the task *as a team* in thirteen seconds.

It is beautiful to watch group members bring their best individual talents and positive attitudes toward a common goal.

> **WINNING IS GOOD. WINNING WITH OTHERS IS BEST.**

By risking individual accolades and invincibility, an unforeseen greater outcome is achieved. Winning is good. Winning with others is best.

What separates people? What separate teams?

- distrust

- fear of personal risk

DISTRUST

We all have influence, and we have a choice whether our influence is positive or negative. While we cannot expect those in positions of authority to be perfect, we can and should expect them to honor the privilege and responsibility of having others follow them. We need more leaders who are not only competent and committed to excellence but are also caring. A leader's power to influence is grounded in caring.

No one knows the mind-set of leaders better than Marshall Goldsmith. He is often labeled as the top executive-leadership coach in the world. I am certified in his methodology because I believe in his methods and philosophies completely. In his best-selling book *What Got You Here Won't Get You There*, Goldsmith teaches us that leader effectiveness is less about what to do and more about what not to do. By *what not to do*, he is referring to interpersonal behaviors. He suggests that the higher up the ladder leaders go, behaviors (people skills) become both more important and more potentially problematic than those leaders' job talents or capabilities. Here are five of Goldsmith's twenty "transactional flaws" that leaders can perform against others:

- **Passing judgment:** The need to rate others and impose our standards on them.

- **Making destructive comments:** The needless sarcasm and cutting remarks that we think make us sound sharp and witty.

- **Starting responses with "no," "but," or "however":** The overuse of these negative qualifiers secretly says to everyone, "I'm right. You're wrong."

- **Refusing to express regret:** The inability to take responsibility for our actions, admit we're wrong, or recognize how our actions affect others.

- **Not listening:** The most passive-aggressive form of disrespect for colleagues.

I imagine we quickly recognize many of these behaviors in bad bosses we've had, but do we recognize these behaviors in ourselves? I've certainly done them. Each of these behaviors, individually and collectively, intended or not, tell another person that we don't care. Trust and performance outcomes are at stake. The quality of our relationships is in direct proportion to the intentions and personal accountability we bring to them.

If we are to be Caring Warriors, we have to be conscious of our influence. How can we . . .

- expect those we influence to learn if we are not learners?

- expect others to be committed if we are not committed?

- express the importance of trust if we ourselves are not trustworthy?

- ask others to set goals if our priorities and personal goals are unclear?

- demand respect if our actions and words don't demonstrate respect?

- call for better communication if we don't listen?

- assess another's behaviors if we lack self-awareness or a desire to improve?

- expect openness and honesty if we lie or omit important truths?

- ask our people to help other teammates if we are selfish?

- demand another's time if we do not respect the value of that individual's time?

- expect others to fight for us if we're not willing to fight for them?

TRUST IS RISKY

In the absence of an environment of trust and collaboration, even with people they know, human beings naturally revert to the fixed, scarcity-centric mind-set of safety and survival. Consider how we're likely to behave in the first meeting with a new group, new team, or new neighbor. We have our guard up; we mask our feelings. Very little of who we really are is visible. Why? We want to be perceived as capable, poised, smart, and "tough enough" to be safe in what we perceive as an unsafe environment. We are afraid, and as a result, we are not at our best. Instead of thinking, *Nothing ventured, nothing gained,* we say to ourselves, *Nothing risked, nothing lost.*

In our work lives, we may keep our masks on, waiting to see where we land in the perceived pecking order. Not knowing where we stand and not feeling safe, we feel continuously under threat. Then, as an example, an underprepared or flat-out wrong person is put in an authority role. He or she becomes our boss. These "leaders" model self-centeredness and insecurity when they feel compelled to put undue pressure on their team to mask their incompetence. *All for me* and *me for me* is how these leaders think and behave. Consequently, we do not feel safe nor trust.

Me thinking keeps us separate. We are all looking over our shoulders, never quite able to relax and do our best work for the good of the group. And why should we? No one cares about us, right? We're never able to fill the cups of validation and approval. We perform below our capacity as individuals, teams, and organizations. We lower our expectations of ourselves and our teams. Think of the incredibly talented work teams and sports teams you know that underperform when they should dominate.

ME THINKING KEEPS US SEPARATE.

Individuals in groups and teams who don't feel cared about do not feel empowered to perform at the top of their game. They persist in a constant suboptimal state, characteristic of survival and protection. It's too risky to put everything on the line for leaders and others who won't do the same for us, so performance and fulfillment suffer.

PEOPLE ARE CONNECTED BY CARING INFLUENCE

We are only able to connect with people and have a positive influence if they know that we care and that they can trust us. Legendary football coach Lou Holtz shares his similar wisdom. One of his golden rules is, *show people you care.* Holtz says there are three fundamental questions others ask themselves in every interaction. They are:

1. Can I *trust* you? "Without trust, there is no relationship... Without trust, you don't have a chance. People
   have to trust you."

2. Are you *committed* to excellence? People will trust
   you and follow you if you are committed to doing
   your very best.

3. Do you *care* about me? Lou says, "Caring about
   people is enabling them to be successful."[8]

So *caring*, *trust*, and *commitment* are triplets. Each intimately ties in
with the others. You cannot have trust without commitment, and
you cannot have trust without caring. For example, if you think that
your boss is not committed to you and your teammates, then your
belief is that he doesn't care. Goodbye, trust. Goodbye, best effort
and loyalty. You get the point.

Relationships exist in a constant storm of intentions and interpretations. When intention and interpretation match up, we say,
"We're on the same page. We're simpatico." When intentions do
not match interpretations, we have a disconnect. We have what is at the
center of every sitcom ever written: *misunderstandings*. I am obsessive
about trying to explain my inten-
tions, and I still regularly fail. It's

> "WE JUDGE OURSELVES
> BY OUR INTENTIONS
> AND OTHERS BY THEIR
> BEHAVIOR."

important to point out that "We judge ourselves by our intentions
and others by their behavior."[9] We assume that we're accurately

---

8   Harvey Mackay, "Lou Holtz's 3 Rules of Life," May 10, 2012, http://harveymackay.
com/column/lou-holtz's-3-rules-of-life/.

9   Stephen Covey, *The Speed of Trust: The One Thing That Changes Everything* (Free
Press, 2006).

assessing meanings as receivers and accurately delivering intentions as communicators. It's amazing that any of us can navigate the matrix of communication. It takes great effort. Our influence and connection depends upon our batting average with intention and interpretation. We can't control others' intentions or behavior, but we can observe and work on our own. Caring Warriors—leaders—care enough to work at it. We can improve our batting average.

Here are a handful of mismatch examples from a work setting. Clearly in relationships, they can be even more intense.

INTENTION	INTERPRETATION
(looking down at his phone) I'll finish this last e-mail/text before I begin this next conversation.	He doesn't respect me or my time.
I'll send a quick e-mail letting Stacy know that I want to talk to her before she leaves the office.	He didn't explain why he wants to meet. I must be in trouble.
We need to discuss our low sales performance. I'm calling a meeting Wednesday before Thanksgiving, because we need to get focused. This will instill a sense of urgency.	Nothing is ever good enough. She only cares about how our sales performance impacts her reputation. Can't it wait until Monday morning?
I better make an example of Bob at our next team meeting to demonstrate that I won't tolerate anything less than excellence.	He is despicable. Here I am, going through the worst time in my life, and he's on my butt. Not only does he call me out publicly, but he isn't aware of the extra communicating and planning I'm doing with my colleagues behind the scenes to manage everything.
I really want this new deal to work. I have to keep people focused and engaged. I'm not going to indulge in a lot of discussion with people about the changes.	She has no interest in our feelings or how these changes affect us. I can't get behind her.

WHAT ARE SOME OF YOUR MISMATCHES?

INTENTION	INTERPRETATION

WHEN INTENTIONS GO WRONG

Reorganization always comes on the heels of an acquisition; that means new faces in leadership positions, and it's typically very tumultuous for everyone, at every level. After one of many acquisitions, my new boss, a senior executive, asked me to arrange a dinner with two of my most experienced direct reports. I thought this was a great idea: an opportunity for my team to interact and grow. I said to him, "How about if I step out so they can spend time with you? I want them to feel empowered. I want them to feel special. It's an opportunity for them to learn, and I don't want them to even have the temptation to defer to me as their boss."

My boss insisted that I be there. He said, "I really respect them. I want to get their feedback on how things are going with the recent changes. I want you to come. It'll be great. We'll have fun."

Betsy and Ava were great contributors and admirable working moms. Both had families and busy lives they put on hold for the evening to spend time with the "big boss." They'd soon wish that they had stayed home.

Several margaritas in, my boss asked, "Let me hear some feedback. How are things going? You two are the best of the best. I want to hear what's going well and what isn't. How are we doing in these first ninety days?" Fair enough—the women got into it, honestly and openly, because he'd asked, and they thought he really wanted to hear it.

That's when things got uncomfortable; all of a sudden his body language tightened. He was offended. I could see that he had taken their thoughtful feedback personally because he was part of making some of those decisions, and he was trying to change things. The women were powering on with their observations, unaware of the rumbling volcano. Feeling that things were just about to escalate, I tried to ratchet it all down a little. I said, "All right. This is a healthy conversation we're having. Please pass the chips and queso, por favor."

Suddenly my boss was on his feet, face flushed, cussing them out. To say he was out of control doesn't really cover it; Betsy and Ava were both in complete shock. And at that point, I was no longer his employee or their boss; I was just a man, and this guy was out of line. I grabbed my coat. "Okay. You know what? Dinner's over. Let's get the check." He said something offensive to me—"TJ, your team is negative!"—and the three of us left.

He made half-hearted apologies the following morning, but the damage was done. To the individual, the leader *is* the organization. Maya Angelou said, "People will forget what you said, people will forget what you did, but people will never forget how you made them feel."[10]

---

10 Carmine Gallo, "The Maya Angelou Quote That Will Radically Improve Your Business," Forbes, May 31, 2014, http://www.forbes.com/sites/carminegallo/ 2014/05/31/the-maya-angelou-quote-that-will-radically-improve-your-business/#83693f18d1a9.

In relationships with others, particularly if you're in a position of authority, you have a responsibility to not only develop your self-awareness but also to consider both your intentions and the potential interpretations of your words and behavior. Doing so can prevent irreparable damage.

People mistake the words *awareness, authenticity*, and *personal power* for empty new-age speak. They may suggest that all this fluffy talk doesn't apply to real, day-to-day business leadership challenges. Nothing could be further from the truth. It is exactly when the next words and actions are "high stakes" that awareness and authenticity demonstrate personal power or a lack of it. The story I shared is a perfect example of how positional power (he was a senior vice president) was overshadowed by a gross lack of personal power. His intentions may have been to connect and learn from two of our best, but he failed. His egocentric behavior and lack of awareness that evening left irreparable scar tissue.

The Caring Warrior isn't a wimp; she can talk straight, ask the tough questions, and hold people accountable, but she is also aware of how she may come across to others. Awareness is personal power: Marshall Goldsmith teaches us what true influencers and role models have in common: ". . . exquisite sense of who they are, which translates into perfect pitch about how they come across to others."[11]

WHO WOULD YOU FOLLOW INTO BATTLE?
WOULD YOU FOLLOW YOU INTO BATTLE?

In the film *We Were Soldiers*, starring Mel Gibson, Keri Russell, and Sam Elliott, a division of air cavalrymen suffers tremendous losses in the early days of Vietnam. The movie begins when they're forming

---

11   Marshall Goldsmith, *What Got You Here Won't Get You There* (New York: Hyperion, 2007).

their teams. To me, this is a parallel to our personal and work lives because we are constantly forming teams and functions based on our ever-changing circumstances.

In one scene in the movie, the lead character (Lt. General Harold G. Moore) and his gunnery sergeant are watching these young officers, taking their teams through training exercises. One of the junior officers is yelling at his team. They're completely exhausted. They're in pain. They've pushed beyond the limit, they're falling down, and he's not even giving them a chance to collect themselves. He's just standing there shouting at them.

In view, not far away, is another junior officer, who has his troopers actually tending to one another's blistered feet, teaching them to care for and about each other, to depend on each other, to see each other as humans and brothers. Caring connects people for the greater good.

> **CARING CONNECTS PEOPLE FOR THE GREATER GOOD.**

HER FEET

I've never attended or watched a Georgia State basketball game, but I would dive into a pool of sharks if GSU's coach Ron Hunter asked me to. Coach Hunter is a general in the army of Caring Warriors. Each year he coaches one of his games in bare feet. Why does he do such a thing? Because he wants to raise awareness for an organization called Samaritan's Feet. Coaching shoeless gets attention, as well it should. To quote the Samaritan's Feet website, "There are 2.2 billion people living in poverty who can't afford education and basic articles of clothing like shoes (World Bank, 2011). Over 1.5 billion people are infected with diseases that are transmitted through contaminated soil (World Health Organization, 2013)."[12]

I had the good fortune of seeing Coach Hunter speak not long ago, and I was moved by his story. He explained that he didn't find Samaritan's Feet—God put it in his path. When he learned about the countless children without shoes, he got involved. His first shoeless game was played, and he made his first trip to Africa with thousands of new shoes in tow. Hundreds of men in the audience teared up as he described to us how his life changed when he washed the feet of a young girl and tied the laces of her first pair of shoes. Hunter told the audience, "I learned that life really isn't about wins and losses, bigger contracts, and notoriety. Life is about giving."

Since 2003, Samaritan's Feet has given over *six million* people a new pair of shoes.[13] Many coaches and leaders have followed Coach Hunter's example and have joined in striving for a world where no children are without shoes.

We influence by caring. Caring connects people. The Caring Warrior fights and leads by *giving*.

"The true way of the warrior is based on humanity, love, and sincerity."

—Morihei Ueshiba, *The Art of Peace*

---

12 Samaritan's Feet, https://www.samaritansfeet.org/our-story/.

13 Ibid.

CHAPTER 5

GIVE

"Life is a gift, and it offers us the privilege, opportunity, and responsibility to give something back by becoming more."

—Tony Robbins

In 1999, my buddy Joe and I went on a ten-hour group climb in the Rockies as part of an Outward Bound program. You should not imagine me, or anyone else in this group, as the ripped and wiry free-climber on the rock face climbing with only Patagonia shorts, a pair of Tevas, and two hands with very strong fingers. God forbid. We were largely a midcareer corporate set. However, this was also no gentle walk up the nature trail. Trust me, I have finished triathlons (rolling across the finish line, mind you). This was *very* challenging.

Our guide, Thor (perfect warrior name!), hit the bullhorn and rustled our group of "city slickers" out of our warm sleeping bags at 2:00 a.m. to lead us up Mt. Elbert. Elbert is not the steepest mountain in the Rockies, but it is the tallest. We were in for a long day.

I had no idea how difficult this climb would be physically, mentally, or emotionally. Thor had reviewed the map and game plan with us the evening before. He told us we would start off in the dark and cold, so we should dress in layers and wear headlamps. He had a checklist and set very specific expectations. As I listened, it felt like I'd had only half an hour of sleep. I was pumped for the climb, but I was also tired and grumpy. I stirred both my coffee and some East Coast sarcasm. Thor (seriously) had a ponytail and years of climbing, guiding, and wilderness expertise, which was super cool, but I also thought of him as kind of a tree-hugging dude. Little did I know how much he would teach me about leadership that day.

The early hours of our long trek were quiet and cold, and that stage of the hike was at a much lower altitude, so the hiking was easy and most of us were just loping along behind Thor. About sixty or ninety minutes in, we stopped for water and a chat. "Hey gang, the incline gets steeper now—it will be more challenging. Look out for your assigned buddy and keep putting one foot in front of the other," Thor said as everyone's eyes opened considerably wider. When we resumed the hike, my friend Joe and I hovered around the rear of the pack. We were surprised to see that Thor also relocated to the back, behind us.

Joe asked Thor, "What made you move to the back?"

Thor responded, "When it's easy at the beginning, I can lead from the front because I know everyone is capable. But when things start getting harder, I move to the back so I can see how people are doing and address any problems from the rear. And if I'm in the back, people are less likely to ask me every twenty minutes how much longer it is until we get to the top or take our next break.

"When the climb gets more challenging, confidence and momentum fluctuate as the reality of fitness levels and of summiting hit home. People struggle, question themselves, and get negative. They have a psychological shift. If people see you in front, they naturally think and act like you're pulling them, and they let up on their effort and initiative.

"But if you set expectations and then observe from the back, they know you're there, but they take responsibility and tend to work harder. They rely more on each other and have an enhanced experience. They get to flex their own leadership muscles. I will move back and forth, mixing and mingling with everyone as a check-in."

> ## SET EXPECTATIONS AND THEN LEAD FROM THE BACK.

Awake now, I noticed Thor moving up and down through the group, sometimes coaching and encouraging people and other times observing from the back.

"Lead from the back and let others believe they are in front."

—Nelson Mandela

UPS AND DOWNS ON THE CLIMB

When you hike for hours, energy and group conversation fluctuate between peaks and valleys. At one point, completely out of nowhere, doing my best Sinatra, I sang "Luck Be a Lady." Everyone laughed. A few people, including Joe, chimed in. When we didn't remember the lyrics, we made up ridiculous words to fit the situation. Someone else belted out some Elvis. Then, for quite a while we tackled an eclectic lineup of songs. We sang Michael Jackson, Journey, U2, Tina Turner, REM, and Marvin Gaye. The most bizarre and unexpected tune came from Thor when he sang (very out of tune) "Bette Davis Eyes" by Kim Carnes. Crazy. Hilarious. What a blast! I said to Joe, "We're in the Colorado Rockies, brother! How cool is this?"

Then the emotional bottom dropped out of the group. After the high of the karaoke session, the energy fizzled and the laughter died down as we approached the final push for the summit. Cue up the gloomy music in a film score. One of the members of our group had fallen. She was fine but complained of sore feet. Briefly back up and moving, she finally had to stop. She had worn the wrong socks (cotton), which made her feet sweat and ultimately caused some nasty blisters. She was tired, in pain, and had the inevitable altitude-sickness headache. She was weepy and grumpy as hell. Come to think of it, we were all winded, ripe, headachy, and "hangry." We had just found our team bottom. Visions of a cold beer and a hotel pool streamed through my mind.

People groaned and paired up to engage in low-voiced complaining and insensitivity toward our fellow climber. She was holding us back—wrong socks, out of shape, passing judgment—and some were speculating about summiting without her. No kidding. The vibe of the moment felt like those times on the TV show *Survivor* where you can't quite hear the whispers, so the producers provide captions of the petty backbiting. What happened to the warrior code of leaving no one behind?

Are neighborhoods, social groups, school activities, and our workplaces that much different? Someone on the team is perceived as not playing along, is not keeping up, or maybe says something on a call or at a meeting that's not taken well. We pounce on that person with a sarcastic text or e-mail to another colleague, and we separate from the larger goal. We forget to *care* and give the benefit of the doubt. The collective morale goes down. Who benefits, really? No one. What about climbing and reaching the summit of the mountain? We were about eight hours in at this point.

Thor to the rescue! Before I tell you what he did, stop for a moment and reflect on the *Survivor* moments in your life. What would you have done in this situation? Bag it? Drop the warrior's sword? Leave her there? Carry her? Just complain and do nothing?

Thor had been listening and observing. He let us flounder in our despair for a little while. Then the Caring Warrior spoke up. As he rubbed first-aid cream on the hobbled hiker's feet, he pulled out an extra pair of synthetic socks he'd brought along just in case. Then he very calmly but directly asked the group, one by one, "Why are you here? Why do you want to get to the top?" After everyone responded, he said, "You all traveled and paid to be here. You all got up in the middle of the night. As great as the view is from the top, you are all here for the experience of doing it. You are trekking in the Rocky Mountains while most of the people you know are in their cubicles or stuck in traffic or whatever. You're sharing this unique experience with others. Dude, you're almost there. Look up. That's the top. Let's go get it!"

We hooted and howled like wolves. Another climber in our group named Juan shouted, "Hell yes!" We all high-fived and hugged. Up we went. Everyone rallied around our comrade with the blisters. We summited in what seemed like ten minutes. Thor had reminded us of our personal intentions, our shared purpose, and our better selves. We rediscovered our positivity and our connection to one another. It felt so much better to be positive. It always does.

At the top, we celebrated and took in the amazing view of the Rockies. It was incredible. Everyone was pumped up and proud. Climbing Mt. Elbert that day was a special memory and experience but an even better lesson in leadership and influence.

THOR'S WARRIOR LESSONS

- Inspire from the front, lead from the back, and coach alongside people.

- Know your *why*, and talk about it early and often (then talk about it some more).

- Have a battle plan and a battle map—show it and review it throughout.

- Be prepared for changing weather—adapt to changing circumstances.

- Remember that, in a group, people have different high points and low points.

- Maintain a realistic and sustainable pace.

- Keep a safe and trusting environment where people can take risks, fail, and grow.

- Show you care when necessary while creating space for initiative to emerge.

- Stop, take breaks, fuel up, check weapons and gear, and review the goal and map.

- Show your team the summit (victory) when you're close. Inspire the last push.

- *Have Fun. Celebrate.*

---

*"Come dance with the west wind and touch on the mountain tops.
Sail o'er the canyons and up to the stars.
And reach for the heavens and hope for the future and all that we can be and not what we are."*

—John Denver, "The Eagle and the Hawk"

PUT OTHERS FIRST

A Caring Warrior is a guardian. In his book *Leadership: The Warrior's Art,* Christopher Kolenda described the warrior as "one who possesses the highest ethics and morals, who is kind, respectful, and caring toward society, comrades in arms, and noncombatants, and yet fully trained and ready to fight…"

Eddie Williams, US senior vice president at Novo Nordisk, was the executive who first developed me as a leader. His mantra is, "Always put your people first. Then everything else will take care of itself." He lived it. Eddie had hundreds of people reporting to him, a calendar full of meetings, and many shifting priorities competing for his attention. Yet in my first week as a new manager, he cleared his entire schedule for two full days to train and develop me. *Two full days.* Many people have shared with me over the years that they've barely spent two minutes with a senior leader, let alone two days.

So what did we do with that time? First, we got to know one another. I'll bet we spent half of the first day discussing our backgrounds, personal philosophies, and professional experiences. Then we talked about expectations. He discussed the importance of clear and high expectations. The caveat though, he taught me, is that you cannot set expectations for others if you don't have high expectations of yourself and if you aren't willing to ask what your people expect of you. In order to lead others, one has to know what they need and want. Then the Caring Warrior cares enough to deliver on those expectations. Both parties in the relationship have to respect what I call a "Contract 4 Success."

We shook hands and agreed to move forward holding one another accountable with the best intentions and expectations. With our remaining time, Eddie taught me everything he knew about our market, our customers, and our industry. He changed the way I thought about leadership forever because he put *me* first. By working with me as a new manager, he was helping equip me to better help others. By caring enough to give me his time and attention and putting me first, Eddie earned my trust and commitment. He also set me on the right path to improving my competence.

> *"Leadership starts with having the sincere desire to help others grow personally and professionally. This must be the joy we feel when those we have helped (even in the smallest way) reach their full potential. However, the greatest joy comes when they do the same for others—pay it forward. Then, you have truly made a difference."*
>
> —Eddie Williams

So what does it mean in practice to "put your people first"? You have to meet people where they are and give them the gifts of time and attention. I told you earlier about Ashley, the new manager who had trouble with her team. She only became effective with her people when she prioritized the individuals on her team. The great irony of putting others first is that by choosing the selfless approach, you get much more in return. Here I am writing about Eddie Williams in a book sixteen years after he promoted and developed me. He has hired, promoted, and developed hundreds of leaders in his industry; some still work with him directly, and many have gone on to achieve their own success in other companies and professions. Humbly and unknowingly, Eddie created a tribe of Caring-Warrior leaders who are paying it forward.

WE FOLLOW LEADERS WHO CAN PUT OTHERS FIRST

Rohit, a sales manager I worked with, promoted Jake, a middle-range performer who had a talent for strategy and impressive knowledge of the marketplace. Jake made market research, competitive war games, and intel gathering his hobbies. He shared his knowledge with his team. He was also the go-to team member for message accuracy and marketing materials. In-house product managers valued Jake's input. Rohit saw all this potential, and in spite of Jake's mediocre sales performance, he pushed to promote him into a marketing position. Jake was a superstar in his new role. He moved up that channel and ended up in a much higher-level position than Rohit, his support-ive boss. Jake could easily have fallen through the cracks or worse, been discarded as not worth developing, but he deserved an oppor-tunity. Rohit cared enough to get behind Jake and help him realize his potential.

CONTRACT 4 SUCCESS

I was fortunate to get off on the right foot with a great leader and mentor who cared to get to know me and to set expectations. It surprises me how underestimated both caring and expectations are. When we care about a person, a goal, an event, a cause, or a new opportunity, we have expectations. And don't the other people involved have their own expectations? Then why do we talk about them so little? I can't answer that. Mismanaged and undiscussed expectations have wreaked havoc in my life as well (many times my fault). But I do have a very effective and simple approach with new colleagues and team members that could help in all aspects of your life. I call it the Contract 4 Success. Think of it as a pre-endeavor, prerelationship agreement. You can, and should, call it whatever you like and whatever fits your situation. I'll briefly explain how it works, and then I'll show it to you.

My Contract 4 Success is an agreement in the form of a written template where two parties discuss their four most important expectations for the relationship, whether that relationship is manager, employee; teammate, teammate; teacher, student; roommate, roommate; or whatever fits your situation. Each person takes a turn speaking and writing their "big four" expectations. They talk through and clarify understanding on each expectation, which often leads to a very rich conversation, agreement, and the act of both people signing the document. Connect. Communicate. Commit.

Here is an of the template in a manager, direct-report situation:

Scenario: I recently hired Sara as a manager of training and development. Sara and I got to know one another well during the interviewing process, and I am confident that she has the skills and abilities to perform the job exceptionally well. I believe that she will enhance the team and will also lift up the organization as a future leader. She has recently completed onboarding/orientation at the organization, and today is our first sit-down meeting together. Our goal is to set expectations, then discuss her professional goals, and finish with the immediate priorities of her role. First, I give Sara the opportunity to tell me her expectations of me.

CONTRACT 4 SUCCESS

Name: _____ Date: _____

Expectations

☐

☐

☐

☐

_____

Name: _____ Date: _____

Expectations

☐

☐

☐

☐

CONTRACT 4 SUCCESS

Name: _Sara Sample_____ Date: _10/10/2016_____

Expectations

☐ Clear direction on my responsibilities/priorities.

☐ Reasonable timeframe to get up to speed (TBD and discussed).

☐ Honesty and straightforward feedback.

☐ Some flexibility in my morning start. I have to drop daughter at school every morning at 8:30 am, which means I can't get here until 9:00 am.

Name: _TJ Jones_____ Date: _10/10/2016_____

Expectations

☐ Commitment to excellence by making internal stakeholders a priority. Communicate with them at least weekly if not more.

☐ Trust me and give me the benefit of the doubt when I seem stressed or distant. I commit to always keeping you informed when I can.

☐ Honesty about the good, the bad and the ugly. I trust your abilities but I need to stay informed because I'm asked often where things stand when my team isn't present.

☐ We have a thankless job sometimes. Stay positive and save any stress or negativity for me and the team. We serve the entire executive team and the company. They will trust us if we do everything with excellence and with positivity.

The point is simple—but far too often, this conversation never happens. Any more than four big expectations is too many and increases the chances of breaking the contract and not living up to the agreement. The point isn't to make this legally binding (which it will never be) or punitive but to have an honorable agreement among adult human beings. Care enough to have the conversation—it will improve your influence, your relationships, and your outcomes.

CARING ALIGNS AND INSPIRES PEOPLE

Caring leaders hold people accountable without stripping them of their dignity. Caring leaders navigate change with grace. Caring leaders know who they are and help others to see who they are. Caring leaders are humble in success and strong during times of failure or difficulty. Caring leaders approach influence and leadership as though it were an art form. My high school football coach, Mike Haugh, made caring leadership look like art.

Leaning against the cold cement of the outer gymnasium wall, I felt the bass vibration of loud music against my back. *Thump, thump. Wom, wub, wub. Thump, thump. Wom, wub, wub. Thump, thump. Wom, wub, wub.* At first, I thought someone from our team had brought in a stereo. But that wasn't what we did before games. We talked game strategy, then most of us stayed quiet getting ready for the upcoming game.

I realized the music was coming from the parking lot as the screeching brakes of an old school bus converged with the thumping percussion. Our opponents, the Charlotte football team, arrived in bold style. They had the attention of everyone within a few miles. They certainly had my attention. My heart thumped. My hands shook. I was nervous. No, I was scared. I hadn't slept well the previous night, and I'd spent most of the morning in the bathroom.

Charlotte, my father's alma mater, was known to be a tough and intimidating city school. They produced top athletes, and in football they had greater size, speed, and talent. The Charlotte team that year was undefeated, as were we, but they had racked up record-breaking yardage on offense and had held other teams to less than ten points scored. We didn't dare say it out loud, but we were freaking out.

My hometown, Livonia, just south of Rochester, New York, is a warm and friendly small-town community. At that time, each graduating class had around one hundred students in it, which is pretty small for a public school. We did well in sports, particularly when we played other similar-sized schools from "the country." I was a five-foot-ten quarterback who also played in the band and performed in musicals. I wasn't feeling very tough at that moment, and I wasn't sure I'd ever sing another show tune after that day. As the bus parked, I heard a shout: "Coming after your ass, Jones!" Gulp. His teammates joined in with more obnoxious, loud curses and insults to everyone within earshot of the bus.

Sensing our declining mood and confidence, Coach Haugh pulled us into a large standing huddle. I remember that we were standing because nearly all of us were taller than him. He was a feisty and noble warrior at five foot seven, the kind of person who commands respect without trying—and with very few words. He could see the fear in our eyes. He looked up with a flaming red face and said in a low, calm voice: "Boys, I just realized that we will beat this team today whether we have a higher score on the board or not. We will beat them with our honor. They have come to our home, disrespected our town, our school, and our families with their behavior. We will show them how young men are supposed to act and play on the football field. We will beat them with our discipline. On every play, between whistles, we will break their spirit with our intensity and drive, because we won't stop. We will come after them *by the book, by the rules,* surprising them with our endurance right up until the last play of the game. When we knock them down, after the play we'll reach out and offer a hand to pick them up. We'll smile before each snap, and we'll smile when the play is over. We'll beat them with our brand of football. More importantly, we'll beat them with how we behave." He paused, looked over his shoulder at the field, then returned to look at us—a slight moisture in his eyes—and finished with, "Now let's go teach them how to behave when they come to our home."

We beat them fourteen to zero. I don't remember the details of the game, but I remember that pregame speech. I remember the way my teammates and I conducted ourselves during the game as the other team got flustered and frustrated. They yelled at one another and cursed at the referees throughout. None of my teammates nor I participated in any fights or shoving matches. I saw my buddies grabbing hands and showing sportsmanship. We were perfect gentleman. We had grace. Coach couldn't give us more height, more speed, or more talent. What he gave us was a lesson in character. Our noble behavior that day won over our opponents, too. Many of us walked off the field that afternoon wishing one another well. We had other big wins that season, but that one sticks with me above all the others, because our coach cared enough to remind us of who we were and who we wanted to be: honorable men. Care enough to bring the best out in yourself and in others.

> **CARE ENOUGH TO BRING THE BEST OUT IN YOURSELF AND IN OTHERS.**

CHAPTER 6

INFLUENCE

"Warmth is the conduit of influence: It facilitates trust and the communication and absorption of ideas."

—Amy Cuddy

My new work team exchanged messages back and forth, trying to decide what we would do to celebrate the Christmas holiday. Would we exchange presents? Go out to dinner? Send a gift basket and be done with it? Did people even want to get together? Being a new manager, this was a surprisingly stressful decision. I wanted the input of all twelve members of the team, mostly because I wanted them to remember this year together, and I had no ideas myself.

Luckily, I had a Caring Warrior on my team. Bill Loftus was a legend in our ranks, a man literally loved by every customer or colleague he ever met. I was his manager, but Bill was my teacher. He called me to chat and share his thoughts on the Christmas party. He said, "TJ, it sounds like there are a lot of ideas floating around, and you're putting a lot of pressure on yourself to pick that perfect blend of fun, holiday cheer, and a meaningful experience. With your permission, I'd like to recommend something for you to consider." What a gentleman!

I said, "Bill, absolutely. Please. What do you suggest?"

Two weeks later, the week before Christmas, all thirteen of us walked down the street carrying a Christmas tree, decorations, and piles of presents for a family who needed a little kindness. I remember the grateful faces on the man and woman when they greeted us at the door. They hugged every one of us as we set up the tree and handed them the other items.

Our team went out for coffee and bagels later that morning. All of us were aglow. No steak dinner or team activity could have surpassed the feeling of goodwill and closeness our team felt that Christmas. I love Bill for teaching me that lesson and for being a Caring Warrior.

WHAT DOES THE CARING WARRIOR LOOK LIKE AS A FRONTLINE MANAGER?

I've been lucky enough to work with quite a few Caring Warriors. Mendy Shaw Ringer stands out to me because she focused on the well-being and development of her people first and foremost. Mendy was like a business-world Reese Witherspoon. She could do it all: sell, market, train, hire, sing (no kidding), collaborate, and last but not least, lead. Mendy always had a smile on her face. She lifted up her team and the people around her. She inspired. Sure, she questioned things at times, but she never went dark and never succumbed to whining, cynicism, or gossip. Her teams absolutely loved and respected her because they knew she cared about them. She was smart and competent in her role, but she put her people first. During leadership meetings with senior executives, Mendy always had the courage and grace to ask questions about how decisions and changes affected people first, then business. At larger company meetings, you could tell who was part of her team because they carried themselves with positivity and wanted to be with one another and with their leader. Mendy's influential magic was *giving* herself to her team.

CARE ENOUGH TO STEP BACK AND LET OTHERS LEAD

Very few of the training and team-building engagements I've done have included senior leaders; ironically, it is often the executives who sign off on the initiative, yet they don't take the time or make the effort to participate. But I once had a team of UPS senior leaders in an outdoor-experiential course. It was a transformative day. This was a group of leaders who genuinely wanted to collaborate, but at the outset, you could tell they were reticent to speak up with ideas and suggestions because their collective boss, the company's US president, was also participating (and was wearing jeans and a sweatshirt). I was impressed and thrilled that he was there rolling up his sleeves, but I could see that his mere presence cast a heavy cloak over the problem-solving initiatives. A dynamic personality, the other senior leaders deferred to him on final decisions and tactics.

Midmorning, exasperated, he finally said, "I don't have all the answers! I'm just here to participate. We're all a team. Speak up. We'll get to better solutions if everyone jumps in. Most of you are smarter and better educated than me anyway. Lighten up and have some fun." That's how you do it—humbly, collectively, inclusively. I heard sighs, observed heads shaking, and I could see everyone's shoulders drop. What a crucial and unexpected moment in the day. I wish I had planned it myself, but it changed the energy and the value of the initiative. And we had a lot of fun too. This group let their hair down. My stomach hurt from laughing so hard. We climbed, jumped, lifted, built, and learned.

At the end of the day we reviewed the lessons. Here are a few of the takeaways: The first idea is rarely the best—get everyone involved to surface the best solutions to a problem. Invest more time in the beginning of a challenge (project/initiative) planning the strategy—it makes execution more efficient. Adapt to failures and setbacks without blaming—it wastes time and energy.

We ended the day on the sand volleyball court. The experience that day truly bonded and transformed that leadership team. Their president set a great example of how to influence and integrate a team by humbly stepping back so others could step forward.

BUILD AND EMPOWER A HEROIC TEAM

Establish an identity. Get to know the unique qualities and similarities of the individual team members—talk about them as a group. Maybe give yourselves a cool name? You may even want to have a team logo. Every team I've led has had an identity and a name. One group I worked with in the Southeast called itself "the Hurricanes." We had a logo, T-shirts, hats—all of it. We called ourselves the Hurricanes because in our collective view

- hurricanes, like us, are often underestimated in their power;

- we get faster and stronger, building momentum;

- we learn and pick things up along the way; and

- in the South, Hurricanes should always be on the radar.

This may sound corny to you, but trust me and give it a try. Go 'Canes!

Establish a team creed. Your creed describes your methods of operating, communicating, behaving, or functioning. Your creed is not a list of goals; it is a group commitment for how you will work together. It is your team's spirit. By establishing a team creed, you are setting the stage for accountability, trust, and enduring performance. Here is an example creed:

- We will **perform at our best** every day in our individual positions and efforts to be successful for our loved ones, our team, and ourselves.

- We will **speak positively** to one another and give one another the **benefit of the doubt.**

- We will **"deal direct."** We will speak directly to the person we may be having a challenge with versus **talking behind one another's backs.**

- We will **celebrate** each other's and our own victories and successes, large or small.

- We will **share** ideas and best practices.

- We will demonstrate **integrity**, representing our team, our organization, and ourselves in an honest and honorable way.

"When you hire amazing people and give them freedom, they do amazing stuff."

—Seth Godin, *Tribes: We Need You to Lead Us*

Engage and connect the right people. Connect and surround yourself with positive, energetic, capable, and caring people. Bathe in the glow of winning behaviors.

Here are a few traits that I think constitute winning behavior (in no particular order):

- positivity and enthusiasm

- skill—talent and potential to improve

- work ethic

- leadership behaviors

- desire to learn and grow

- self-awareness and composure

- connection skills—communication and relationships

- spirit and fun

CONNECT AND SURROUND YOURSELF WITH POSITIVE, ENERGETIC, CAPABLE, AND CARING PEOPLE.

Fortune magazine interviewed sixteen of the hiring managers from the "100 Best Companies to Work For" survey of 2014. Here is what a few of these top company representatives had to say about hiring:

- "We want to get to know the candidate as a person, not just as a set of technical skills. Great candidates are the ones that come in prepared to engage us in conversation, ask us great questions, and are authentic. We have extensive training for employees to learn technical skills, but we cannot teach people to provide genuine heartfelt care to others."

—Stephanie Troxel, director, diversity & recruitment, Kimpton Hotels & Restaurants

- "We are looking for people who aren't afraid to be themselves, don't take themselves too seriously, and are constantly looking to improve both personally and professionally."

  —Mike Bailen, recruiting manager, Zappos.com

- "I'm always impressed by candidates who have taken the time to visit one of our stores during the interview process—and who have visited our *What We Stand For* blog to understand more about our culture and leadership style. That kind of curiosity and attention to detail is a great fit for our company."

  —Eva Gordon, VP of stores, training, development, and recruiting, The Container Store[14]

Hiring and engaging with others is like a dating relationship. Treat it that way. Spend time talking about a variety of subjects, not just work or what you have in common. Get to know the individual in different settings and circumstances. See how they interact with others. Talk about the mistakes and triumphs of the past. Review opportunities for improvement. Find out what you both want for the future. Discuss how you want the (working) relationship to be. Introduce this potential new person in your life to "the family": your team, your colleagues, and the people whose opinion you respect.

I'm amazed at how little time is spent making hiring decisions. Sticking with the dating analogy, if you have some basic chemistry

---

14 Christopher Tkaczyk, "16 great secrets from Best Companies recruiters," *Fortune*, January 16, 2014, http://fortune.com/2014/01/16/16-great-secrets-from-best-companies-recruiters-fortunes-best-companies-to-work-for/.

with someone but your family and friends see red flags, then you have some brakes to pump and some thinking to do. Take your time.

There is no degree, aptitude test, pedigree, connection, or superficial quality that can triumph over a mismatch in values. We are all wonderfully unique, with gifts to offer the groups of our lives. But if we compromise our values and instincts when we hire, make friends, or chose our partners, we diminish the value of our life.

> WE ARE ALL WONDERFULLY UNIQUE, WITH GIFTS TO OFFER THE GROUPS OF OUR LIVES. BUT IF WE COMPROMISE OUR VALUES AND INSTINCTS WHEN WE HIRE, MAKE FRIENDS, OR CHOSE OUR PARTNERS, WE DIMINISH THE VALUE OF OUR LIFE.

To pull a concept from Jim Rohn, one of the most frequently quoted motivational self-help gurus: We become the people we are around the most. Our professional and personal fulfillment and success directly correlate.

PROFESSIONAL LIFE

- Our team becomes the people we hire and promote.

- Our team becomes the individuals we reward and recognize.

- Our culture becomes the people we develop as future leaders.

- Our morale reflects the people we give the stage (voice) to.

- Our professional fulfillment and achievement derive from the quality of mentors and influences we surround ourselves with.

- Our level of influence with our teams and organizations is the result of the choices we make to care for and give to others.

PERSONAL LIFE

- The most important choices we make in life are to

  □ awaken to and love who we are;

  □ choose who we will love and give our heart to;

  □ serve the world with our gifts, art, and genius; and

  □ select the mentors who will teach and influence us to be more.

- We cannot choose the people we have to interact with every day, but we can choose the influence we allow them to have on our thinking, personality, and decisions.

- We are shaped by the people we spend the most time with, and so the same can be said in reverse. We factor in to what others become. What impact are we having?

> **WE CANNOT CHOOSE THE PEOPLE WE HAVE TO INTERACT WITH EVERY DAY, BUT WE CAN CHOOSE THE INFLUENCE WE ALLOW THEM TO HAVE ON OUR THINKING, PERSONALITY, AND DECISIONS.**

"Do not hire a man who does your work for money, but him who does it for the love of it."

—Henry David Thoreau

EMPOWER MILLENNIAL TALENT

"Despite struggling with debt, recession, and the jobs crisis, millennials—who will account for 75% of the workforce in 2025—are not motivated by money. Rather, they aim to make the world more compassionate, innovative, and sustainable.

More than 50% of millennials say they would take a pay cut to find work that matches their values, while 90% want to use their skills for good.

The future of work lies in empowering millennial talent. Deloitte's 2015 Millennial Survey found that 7,800 future leaders from 29 different countries say the business world is getting it wrong. Some 75% say they feel businesses are focused on their own agendas rather than improving society, while only 28% say they feel their current organization is making full use of their skills."[15]

Millennials want what we all want. They want effective leaders who care, who inspire, and who have a positive influence on their careers and lives. They want to be valued for their unique skills, ideas, and potential. They want to be accountable and to be coached, but they want you to treat them like human beings, not human capital.

This generation is about honest and open communication. Effective leaders set the example when they involve their people in respectful conversation, encouraging creativity rather than suppressing it for some agenda. If you give people you're coaching and leading a chance to be heard, you may bring out better ideas and better

---

15   Adam Smiley Poswolsky, "What Millennial Employees Really Want," Fastcompany.com, June 4, 2015, http://www.fastcompany.com/3046989/what-millennial-employees-really-want.

solutions than the ones that you have. And even if a better solution doesn't surface, you're still giving them that respect and opportunity.

Navigate your future. If you want to boldly sail into the future, you will need to center your boat's MAST. How is the millennial generation like the mast of a boat?

- It holds the lookout position for dangers and new destinations.

- The direction of the sail (the boom) pivots on the mast.

- The waters could get rough on your trip, but the mast will be the core of the ship.

SUCCESS WITH MILLENNIALS = MAST

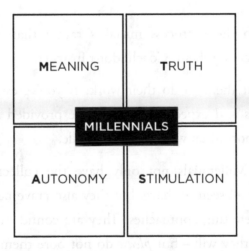

Meaning: Millennials have been exposed to unprecedented amounts of violence, technological advancement, and social upheaval and conscientiousness. While they get tagged with a reputation for superficiality and narcissism, the truth is that they want to make a positive difference in the workplace and in the world. It is not enough to just give orders and point at the hill. This group needs to understand *why*.

- Consider your purpose, and explain it.

- Include meaning and positive contribution in your messaging and communication.

- Provide feedback that speaks to contribution and purpose in addition to coaching on skills and competencies.

Autonomy: Like generation Xers, millennials not only prefer space and autonomy, they demand it, dude! Seriously, with speedy access to information and solutions, you would be wise to not micromanage or hover. I'm not sure anyone responds well to someone breathing down his neck.

- Be clear in your communication. Then, let them give it a try.

- Help them process mistakes rather than stopping and correcting them. Coach, don't instruct.

- Trust them to do their work. If you've established clear goals and expectations and have provided resources and support, then watch, don't meddle.

Stimulation: Millennials not only have the collective attention deficit that we all seem to have, but they also crave new challenges, ideas, and interesting approaches. They are confident they can get it done—and they will—but *please* do not bore them. Keep things interesting.

- Be creative in your project designs and methods.

- Involve them in discussions about overcoming challenges and making things easier and more efficient.

- Regularly talk about where they are heading in their learning and development. Make sure you connect what they are currently working on or doing with their future goals.

Truth: No BS. This group has seen and heard it all. They won't salute if what you're saying doesn't sound legitimate and authentic. "Because I said so," rarely works with children, let alone adults. Be candid and straightforward but respectful. Give them regular feedback in small doses—just don't act like you're the supervisor in a 1935 steel mill. Talk with them like a human being.

- Tell people what you can, when you can. Help them avoid political landmines. Help them navigate the complexities of the people side of the business, and they will pay you back with their commitment and contribution.

- Keep people informed about where they've been, where they are, and where they're going.

Commit to team goals. Teams are made up of individuals, each with their own goals. So team goals must be limited to just a few. Many teams set too many goals. Too many goals become like alphabet soup, lines on a page, or scrambled eggs. I recommend three very thoroughly fleshed-out goals for shorter periods of time. For example, "In the next ninety days, we . . ." Establish your team goals in the SMART[16] format, which provides clarity and focus.

- S = specific

- M = measureable

- A = attainable

- R = relevant

16   BetterWorks, https://www.betterworks.com/smart-goals/.

- T = time bound

When you write and state goals for yourself or for your teams, state them in the affirmative:

- "I weigh 150 pounds on March 1."

- "At the end of the first quarter, we are ranked number one in sales growth."

- "We finished our project two weeks ahead of time."

Set the execution and accountability bars high. Discussing and writing goals and creeds and team names is great, but it's completely irrelevant if your team is not taking action to achieve and exceed those goals and ambitions. To achieve the individual and team outcomes, each individual must consistently take actions to work toward the goals.

Accountability does not, or *should* not, be limited to a direct line between the leader and the other individual team members. Accountability should flow in every direction across the team. Everyone on the team not only expects the best from him or herself but also from his or her teammates.

In a 2014 *Harvard Business Review* article, Jeanine Prime and Elizabeth Salib presented a good case that humble, altruistic leaders—the ones who are selfless, can listen to criticism, and are willing to learn—are the best leaders. In a study of 1,500 workers from six countries, it was found that the leaders most effective in inspiring loyalty were those who empowered their followers to learn and develop, who took risks personally, professionally, for the greater good, and who treated people respectfully yet consistently held them accountable. Notice that last piece: yes, people want to be held accountable. A Caring Warrior holds people accountable in a respectful and honorable way.

The empowered workers in that study felt included and engaged in their work and with their teams, and that translated to how the teams worked with one another. Workers in these leadership environments helped one another. They felt more creative and innovative, and they went above and beyond the call of duty when other people weren't on the job. Furthermore, altruistic leaders made their people feel a greater sense of uniqueness and belonging.[17] People want to be held accountable by people they trust and whom they know care about them.

Execute in spite of changes. Executing on your goals is a moment-to-moment, day-to-day, week-to-week challenge of endurance, discipline, and adaptability. Individuals and teams that possess the discipline to stay the course, taking action on the agreed-upon behaviors with consistency and a flexibility that adjusts to changing winds and circumstances, will always outperform their counterparts who do not. Bruce Lee is thought to have said, "Notice that the stiffest tree is most easily cracked, while the bamboo or willow survives by bending with the wind."

> PEOPLE WANT TO BE HELD ACCOUNTABLE BY PEOPLE THEY TRUST AND WHOM THEY KNOW CARE ABOUT THEM.

Communicate. We all know communication is important, though we don't always do it enough or effectively. My recommendations here are about *how* and *when* you communicate. I will assume that you already do communicate. *Right?*

- **Discuss and commit to communication and your method.** For example, based on your circumstances, you

---

17   Jeanine Prime and Elizabeth Salib, "The Best Leaders Are Humble Leaders," *Harvard Business Review*, May 12, 2014, https://hbr.org/2014/05/the-best-leaders-are-humble-leaders.

could agree to have a group text, use e-mail predominantly for corporate direction and FYIs, have a weekly call, or plan one-on-one individual calls every Friday at predetermined times.

- **Discuss the frequency of how you as leader will communicate** the team's performance and progress on the team's goals. Five e-mails per day would be ridiculous and annoying, but one update per month is likely too infrequent to stay focused on the goals. Discuss and decide what will work best, and be open to course correction along the way if you see a need to change it. But discuss it, get consensus, and commit.

Connect. **Have fun!** Get people moving, talking, and participating with each other. Create shared experiences. Connecting around shared experiences reminds us that we're all human beings. We are more than our job titles and work output. My most successful teams were the teams who had fun together. They chose to spend time outside of work and had memories of positive work experiences. When did someone decide that work had to be a grind and not a joyful, happy experience? Fun is underrated.

FUN IS UNDERRATED.

Create a "fun department" in your organization. Foremost experts on fun in the workplace Nick Gianoulis and Nat Measley write in their book, *Playing it Forward,* "Fun at work is building solidarity, connection, and an outlet for workplace stress." Gianoulis and Measley recommend replacing the once-per-year forced-fun activity with regular, purposeful, and low-time-commitment fun activities throughout the year.

Doing this will reduce stress, encourage workers to forge connections with each other, and breed an uplifting environment. Furthermore, having regular activities—as opposed to one or two "forced" activities during the year—generally encourages better attitudes and less of an obligatory mind-set. Ten years' experience delivering and teaching companies how to create fun at work has demonstrated the following benefits:

- decreased burnout and boredom

- enhanced creativity and productivity

- increased energy, enthusiasm, and excitement

- improved employee retention and prevention of costly turnover

- improved attraction and retention of the best staff

- boosted profitability[18]

Do you have time for fun? Can you afford it? Can you afford *not* to? Have some fun. *Right now.*

Create a shared story. Effective leaders are the architects of a team's shared story. They facilitate the integration of the team members' collective narratives with a desire and emotional connection for positive change. They help us see a better future. Each team member will be at a different stage of life and career, but each individual has both a personal and group story he or she is a part of. Read, write, edit, embrace, and participate in the stories of the people in your life.

Continue to learn and improve. Human beings, relationships, teams, organizations, and societies are evolving organisms; we have to

---

18   Nick Gianoulis and Nat Measley, The Fun Dept., http://morefunatwork.com/.

continuously grow and develop to continue our success and vitality. Teams that learn together win together.

UNIMAGINABLE GIVING

I am grateful for the servicemen and servicewomen who protect our freedom. The Navy SEALs have team cohesion and a sense of honor and bravery we can all be inspired by. They choose to put others before themselves. Please take in the power of giving.

> **TEAMS THAT LEARN TOGETHER WIN TOGETHER.**

AN EXCERPT FROM THE SEAL CODE: A WARRIOR CREED

"In times of war or uncertainty there is a special breed of warrior ready to answer our Nation's call. A common man with an uncommon desire to succeed...

My Trident is a symbol of honor and heritage. Bestowed upon me by the heroes that have gone before, it embodies the trust of those I have sworn to protect. By wearing the Trident I accept the responsibility of my chosen profession and way of life. It is a privilege that I must earn every day...

The ability to control my emotions and my actions, regardless of circumstance, sets me apart from other men...

Uncompromising integrity is my standard. My character and honor are steadfast. My word is my bond...

We demand discipline. We expect innovation. The lives of my teammates and the success of our mission depend on me—my technical skill, tactical proficiency, and attention to detail. My training is never complete…

In the worst of conditions, the legacy of my teammates steadies my resolve and silently guides my every deed. I will not fail."[19]

Influencing a team, a tribe, or a family is a choice to *give*. Our power to influence manifests when we say to ourselves, *I give it!*

I. G.I.V.E. I.T.

I: INTENTION

Your intention is your aim—your purpose. The true leader has clarity of purpose and a belief that the future can be better for everyone. She accepts that she will make mistakes along the way and have some doubts and uncertainty. In spite of the fear, she continues trusting the call to lead and trusting her purpose. She accepts responsibility, believing that she will serve and inspire others along the way.

There's no better time than the present to be a positive influence on others.

A Caring Warrior sets him or herself an intention: *I can lead and influence with an open and wise heart, and good things will come for others and for me. I can maintain high expectations of myself and others. And I can pursue my goals and ambitions with others, not at their expense.*

G: GOALS

If we just "show up" for our most cherished and immediate relationships, we compromise them. Either we are growing in those relation-

---

19 "SEAL Ethos/Creed," Naval Special Warfare Command, http://www.public.navy. mil/nsw/Pages/EthosCreed.aspx.

ships, or the connection weakens. The Contract 4 Success is a great place to start, even in personal relationships. Have the conversation about expectations and what you want to achieve together. Don't leave it up to chance. Examples:

- **Spouse or life partner:** Set goals for how you want to be in the relationship, how you will speak to one another, things you want to do, and places you want to go.

- **Professional, athletic, or artistic collaborator:** Set goals for the outcomes of your time working together on temporary or ongoing projects. How will we be, and what will we accomplish?

- **Manager or leader:** Set mutual goals for a positive and productive relationship. I didn't have all the answers or control of my direct reports' futures, but I cared enough to want them to develop their talents and grow. I wanted the experience of working with me to be a positive experience—not all lollipops and rainbows, but still life enhancing.

I: INQUIRY

Ask questions to learn where other people are in their development and mind-set, and then listen. Discover with curiosity what motivates and inspires them. What gets them out of bed in the morning?

V: VALUE

Commit to bringing value to others in every aspect of your life, even those who do not seem to deserve it. The point is doing what you can to realize your best self and serving others with *who you are*. As Seth

Godin writes in *The Icarus Deception,* "The question isn't whether you are capable of godlike work. [You are.] The question is: Are you willing?"

E: EMPATHY

Walk around for a while in someone else's shoes. Imagine what it may be like to be them. We never really know completely what's going on with people. Caring doesn't necessitate that you know someone else's truth. Caring is the gift of trying to understand and wishing them well, hard as it may be at times. Everyone has his own form of suffering and disappointment. Leave room. Everyone has a *reason* and a *season.*

I: INFORMATION

Talk, share, and pay attention. At work, as an authority figure and colleague, don't *assume.* Give people the information to avoid landmines of difficulty, and share the information that will assist them (and you) to learn and make positive progress.

T: TRUST

Ralph Waldo Emerson wrote, "Who you are speaks so loudly, I can't hear what you're saying."[20] Our behaviors—our actions—are the cause, and trust (or the lack thereof) is the effect. Give people a chance to be trusted. Give yourself and others the gift of being trustworthy.

> **GIVE YOURSELF AND OTHERS THE GIFT OF BEING TRUSTWORTHY.**

---

20   Ralph Waldo Emerson, *Self-Reliance and Other Essays* (New York: Dover Publications, 1993).

SUMMARY

- Everyone has influence. Choose to influence positively.

- Strive to do good rather than just look good.

- Caring connects people for the greater good.

- Align intentions with behavior. Individuals judge one another on behavior.

- Mismatches between intentions and interpretations cause the majority of unnecessary conflict.

- The greatest influencers (leaders) know how they come across to others.

- Inspire from the front, lead from the back, and coach side by side.

- Put others first.

- Discuss and agree on expectations with others, both personally and professionally.

- Create a shared story.

- Have fun.

- We influence by giving.

EXERCISES: PERSONAL

POSITIVE INFLUENCE ASSESSMENT

Circle the number on the scale the best represents your self-assessment (1–5). The scores range from 1–5; one (never), two (rarely), three (sometimes), four (often), and five (always).

1. I am a positve person.

Never	Rarely	Sometimes	Often	Always
1	2	3	4	5

2. I am self-aware and conscious of my intentions in relationships.

   1   2   3   4   5

3. I am authentic and honest in my interactions with others.

   1   2   3   4   5

4. I am trustworthy.

   1   2   3   4   5

5. I enter relationships open to trusting others until proven otherwise.

   1   2   3   4   5

6. I am generally curious about others, ask questions, and pay attention.

   1   2   3   4   5

7. I work through conflict and misunderstandings with self-control and respect for the other party.

   1   2   3   4   5

8. I am open to changing my view and position when I am wrong.

   1   2   3   4   5

9. I say I'm sorry when I'm wrong and/or out of line in my actions and words.

   1   2   3   4   5

10. I share my creativity, ideas, and solutions for mutual benefit.

   1   2   3   4   5

11. I follow through on my commitments to others.

   1   2   3   4   5

12. I give my best self fully to my relationships.

   1   2   3   4   5

POSITIVE RELATIONSHIP CARING ASSESSMENT
(PERSONAL VISION)

List the 5–10 people who are most important in your life. What is your relationship to that person? Rate yourself on a scale of 1-5: 5=I'm a saint, 4=I go out of my way to give, 3=I demonstrate that I care; 2=I'm harming the relationship; and 1=I'm neglecting the person. I am in jeopardy of losing the relationship.

PERSON	RELATIONSHIP	"I GIVE IT" RATE YOURSELF 1-5

Now, select the three top priority people in your life:

PERSON	WHAT I CURRENTLY DO/DO NOT DO?	WHAT WILL I DO MOVING FORWARD?

How do you generally approach existing relationships? How do you generally approach new relationships? Are you open to new ideas and perspectives?

Do you share your authentic self with the people you interact with?

What quality do you see in yourself that you know is a "blind spot" or a weakness and would feel uncomfortable if anyone knew about you? How can you be kinder to yourself and work through or improve that part of yourself? Who in your life can help you to be better?

What ideas do you have about improving? What will it take to become a better version of yourself?

What positive quality do you possess that others may not be very aware of?

Consider that you are your own mentor. You are the wise, sage leader with years of experience, wisdom, and amazing success. What advice would you give your present self in your relationships with others?

Which three to five qualities have people close to you personally and/or professionally recognized you for or mentioned to you as positive feedback? Do you agree? If so, what is the strongest of your qualities in your view? How can you bring more of that quality to your relationships? How would that conscious effort and awareness enhance your life and those of others you interact with?

What can you change or begin doing right now to enhance your positive influence on others in your relationships?

EXERCISES: PROFESSIONAL

POSITIVE CARING INFLUENCE ASSESSMENT
(PROFESSIONAL VISION)

List the most important roles you play in your work life. Who are the key stakeholders (relationships) that impact your professional success and satisfaction? Rate yourself on a scale of 1–5: 5=I'm a True Caring Warrior, 4=I'm a True Professional, 3=I go along to get along, 2=My relationships with my key stakeholder(s) need to improve ASAP or I have some soul-searching to do about my motivational job fit, 1= I have one foot out the door.

MY ROLE(S)	KEY STAKEHOLDERS	"I GIVE IT" RATE YOURSELF 1-5

Now, select the three most challenging stakeholders (relationships) in your work life:

STAKEHOLDER	WHAT IS CURRENTLY IMPACTING THE RELATIONSHIP POSITIVELY OR NEGATIVELY	POSITIVE SOLUTIONS COURSES OF ACTION

CONTRACT 4 SUCCESS

Name: _____   Date: _____

Expectations

☐

☐

☐

☐

_____

Name: _____   Date: _____

Expectations

☐

☐

☐

☐

Name the roles as influence you have in your life. What are your intentions? How do your intentions change by role? Do they? Is your "identity" in alignment with your intentions toward others? Why or why not?

Who was your best boss (manager) and why? What did he or she do that affected you positively? How did you feel in his or her presence?

Describe the intentions and character traits of this best boss. What positive choices do you believe he or she made in dealing with you that made the difference in your reaction toward him or her?

What qualities in this person do you see in yourself? How do you demonstrate these qualities in your interactions with others?

Consider and describe the worst boss you've had. What did he or she do that affected you negatively? How did you feel in his or her presence?

What qualities in this person do you see in yourself? How do you demonstrate these qualities in your interactions with others?

What trait or quality in your professional life have you most commonly been told is a weakness or area for development?

Consider any strongly held negative beliefs or biases about yourself, the world, or the industry you operate in that may be holding you back. Are these beliefs grounded in truth, or is there a healthier, more positive and productive view? How can you redirect this thinking to improve yourself?

What is it you fear most in your work life? What is the absolute worst thing related to this fear that could happen? If this absolute worst thing happened, how would you respond? What might you learn from such a significant lesson as this?

What is your relationship to learning? How are you with vulnerability? Do you comfortably ask for help? If not, what is at risk? What keeps you from seeking the needed help and counsel that could propel you to the next level?

What is one particular area in your leadership journey where you would benefit *right now* from some valuable input or mentoring? Who could you reach out to for some guidance? Are you ready to take that very important step? Think on it. Write it down. Make a commitment to do it right away.

What does your best look like in your current role? Are you giving it? Have you set yourself apart as a leader—as someone who can be relied upon to perform and step up?

In what ways do you or can you demonstrate leadership (your very best self) in your job description or competencies? How can you improve your interpersonal behavior on your team and in your immediate sphere of influence to make a positive difference for the company, for others, and for yourself?

What immediate action can you take to improve your positive influence?

RESOURCES

BOOKS/ARTICLES

- *Art of Living: The Classical Manual on Virtue, Happiness, and Effectiveness*, Epictetus and Sharon Lebell

- *What Got You Here Won't Get You There: How Successful People Become Even More Successful*, Marshall Goldsmith

- *The Speed of Trust: The One Thing That Changes Everything*, Stephen R. Covey

- *The Art of Peace*, Morehei Ueshiba

- *Leadership: The Warrior's Art*, Chris Cholendra

- Amy J.C. Cuddy, Matthew Kohut, John Neffinger, "Connect, Then Lead," *Harvard Business Review*, July–August 2013, https://hbr.org/2013/07/connect-then-lead

- *Tribes: We Need You to Lead Us*, Seth Godin

- *The Energy Bus*, Jon Gordon

- "Top 100 Companies to Work for" Fortune survey, 2014, http://fortune.com/2014/01/16/16-great-secrets-from-best-companies-recruiters-fortunes-best-companies-to-work-for/

- *Playing It Forward*, Nick Gianoulis and Nat Measley

- "SEAL Ethos/Creed," Naval Special Warfare Command, http://www.public.navy.mil/nsw/Pages/EthosCreed.aspx

- *Self-Reliance*, Ralph Waldo Emerson

- Harvey Mackay, "Lou Holtz's 3 Rules of Life," uexpress, May 7, 2012, http://www.uexpress.com/harvey-mackay/2012/5/7/lou-holtzs-3-rules-of-life

- *The Icarus Deception*, Seth Godin

- Adam Smiley Poswolsky, "What Millennial Employees Really Want," fastcompany, June 4, 2015, http://www.fastcompany.com/3046989/what-millennial-employees-really-want

- Carmine Gallo, "The Maya Angelou Quote That Will Radically Improve Your Business," Forbes, May 31, 2014, http://www.forbes.com/sites/carminegallo/2014/05/31/the-maya-angelou-quote-that-will-radically-improve-your-business/#83693f18d1a9

- Jeanine Prime and Elizabeth Salib, "The Best Leaders Are Humble Leaders," *Harvard Business Review*, May 12, 2014, https://hbr.org/2014/05/the-best-leaders-are-humble-leaders

- "What Are S.M.A.R.T. Goals?" BetterWorks, https://www.betterworks.com/smart-goals/

QUOTES/POEMS/SONGS/ VIDEOS/FILMS

- "People will forget what you said, people will forget what you did, but people will never forget how you made them feel." —Maya Angelou

- Samaritan's Feet website (https://www.samaritansfeet.org/our-story/)

- "The Eagle and the Hawk," John Denver

- *We Were Soldiers*

PART THREE

INSPIRE

BATTLEGROUND: CULTURE.

CALL TO ACTION: INSPIRE EVERYONE
BY SHARING.

CHAPTER 7   CHAPTER 8   CONCLUSION

ENGAGE   **INSPIRE**   **TAKE UP
YOUR SWORD**

*"It takes courage to do those things that people so admire
in great leaders—being vulnerable, admitting a mistake,
apologizing, telling others that we love them, listening, em-
pathizing, abandoning a flawed decision, changing habits
that no longer serve us, standing for integrity and risking
failure and criticism. These all require courage. Doing any of
them inspires others."*

—Lance Secretan, PhD.

CHAPTER 7

ENGAGE

"As a leader you should always start with where people are before you try to take them to where you want them to go."

—Jim Rohn

CARE OR CARE NOT . . . THERE IS NO TRY

"Culture" wasn't a buzzword to Mark McDade; it was part of his moral obligation. McDade was a smart, down-to-earth CEO, a Harvard Business School grad with a strong background in the industry. Mark and his team, with the approval of top investors and the board of directors, acquired a company I was part of in order to expand reach and penetration into more specialized markets and increase profitability with the combined people and products. Even when the business rationale is sound, employees fear loss of jobs, new leadership, and marginalization of their roles. People feel unsettled to say the least.

As chief of a newly blended company, his first instinct was to care about people. Before our first company-wide meeting, he joined his new leadership team for several hours to just "hang out and get to know" us. He asked about our families, our backgrounds. We barely talked about business or work or expectations; he took the time to reassure us that he understood how stressful things had been and to make sure we were okay. In similar circumstances before, I had never experienced that kind of caring and grace. Other CEOs would come to a meeting, give a detached and trite speech, then head straight to the airport without even talking to the leadership team—just in and out. Mark's sincerity connected us to him and to one another.

Later, as he addressed the recently merged organizations from the stage, Mark brought up his first slide: a picture of his family. He said, "Family comes first. If it weren't for them, we wouldn't be able to do what we do, and we wouldn't have the motivation to do what we do." Then he spent a good deal of time talking about developing the talent in the room and the culture, saying, "We're proud to have you be part of it. We want to do right by you—help you to grow and develop."

He meant what he said. Every employee, every role was kept in place. East Coast employees were not required to relocate to the West Coast. Regarding talent and people development, he empowered me to build a comprehensive training and leadership-development platform. He provided resources, and he supported learning and growth. Unlike many senior and midlevel leaders, he regularly attended (and participated in) training and leadership-development sessions my team and I led in different parts of the country. Retention and utilization of training improve when the leaders support the learning and actively participate in it. He always made developing future leaders a priority. In spite of experiencing unsettling change, Mark's caring style immediately inspired us to get to work. I was engaged in Mark's cause from the first day I met him.

In approximately three years postacquisition, as a combined organization, we grew a product valued at $60 million to $250 million. Those three years in that culture were the highest achieving, most fun, and most fulfilling of my career.

Caring works, and it flows downhill from caring bosses who walk the walk. We engage with and give our best to leaders who care.

> **WE ENGAGE WITH AND GIVE OUR BEST TO LEADERS WHO CARE.**

CARING WARRIORS

- care about people first;

- are sincere and real;

- connect people to one another;

- develop and support growth; and

- possess the right heart—the right vision.

"People don't care how much you know until they know how much you care."

—John Maxwell

IN ANOTHER PLACE AND TIME

In the midst of one acquisition and resulting reorganization, we flew in from all over the country for another new leadership team meeting. Those invited to this meeting were the survivors of this major change. There were people from the legacy company, from the original company, and from a new company that it was acquiring. Another new company name, new business cards, new policies, and new idiosyncrasies. More new colleagues.

I had just laid people off on the previous Friday. I had spent the weekend on the phone with all of those friends and colleagues, feeling terrible. I thought to myself, *How many times can this happen in one career?* I hated to see all of those lives and careers disrupted. And what about team and customer relationships? I really grew to hate the whole game of feeling sized up. Often when you're on the receiving end of an acquisition, you aren't able to bring much of a reputation, and regardless of your past contributions, you are starting over yet again. That kind of blank slate may be nice when you transition from high school to college, but it gets old in your career.

Moments such as these are crucial with human beings, who under the circumstances, are naturally hypersensitive to the new vision, mission, and culture. They want to know how the new world will impact their lives. Thus, engagement and trust are fragile concepts, if even possible, because engagement and trust reside in the people who are evaluating their realities. An agenda for the first gathering of a newly blended (merged) large or small organization, like the example I gave previously, should focus on people.

That never happened. We had to be at the office, which some of us had never physically been to before, at 7:00 a.m.

Then the VP came in and said, "Let's talk about culture."

Great, I thought. *We'll have a thoughtful exchange of views on our new culture.* But he jumped right into forty-five minutes of slides. During that time, he told us what the culture would be—his culture. It made sense that part of a performance culture was to have high expectations. I get that. But the majority of the slides were about sales-performance data, bubble charts, and competitive analysis. I wondered when we would talk about culture. After all, my colleagues and I had been very busy over the past months, calming down and communicating with our teams while we delivered excellent performance in the midst of major change. Next slide please.

He said, "This is the performance we expect from you." The atmosphere in the room was tense. He followed up with, "You had an incredible performance last year. But you got lucky. We've told the board that we will grow an additional 15 percent this year."

Then he looked around the room and asked, "What do you all think?" I was quiet—loading up on coffee and looking for a can of gasoline to light myself on fire. Comments from the group were very compliant. He heard what he wanted to hear, so he continued, "We have to stress the sense of urgency with our people, hammer home the goals. We don't have weeks and months to adjust to the new world."

People who had been through this twice in the past three years were now adapting to *another* new set of circumstances. They had new responsibilities, new teammates, new customers, and new, more complicated procedures.

I raised my hand and said, "I'm on board with a high-performance culture. Frankly, every organization I've been in considered themselves that. We absolutely need to know what our objectives are and where we're headed. But I don't think our people would like to hear that they were 'lucky.' They worked hard. We all did. And given the turmoil they've been through with all the change, many spent the past few months worried about the status of their job. Many of their former teammates and friends lost their jobs. There is still a lot of anxiety, even in the people who were asked to stay. It's going to be hard to get them focused until we can redirect how they think and feel." Then I continued cautiously, "Like, are they happy? Since we're talking about culture, *is there something as a leadership team that we can do to excite, reengage, and empower them?*"

Silence. Everyone looked at me like I was from another planet. Or maybe they thought I was from planet Earth but that I needed to be screened for a disorder. Or perhaps they didn't think I was living at all? That's probably it. They saw me there in front of the VP, not as a man or a Caring Warrior but as a carcass being eaten for breakfast on the savannah by a leopard. It's a foggy memory, but I think I said, "Anybody? Guys?" Crickets. Awkwardness. Sweaty brow. Horror. Planning my next step—if I dive through that conference room window, can I roll and survive the landing?

Who cares if they're happy? What does that have to do with anything? On the battleground of culture, decisions being made by people in leadership positions affect others' livelihoods, family lives, stress levels, and health, and that has to be part of the worldview. *Do they care about people?* The new formation of a relationship, team, or organization is an ideal time to set the culture (or fail to). The VP missed the opportunity to set the right tone for culture. From the start, engage and connect people to the cause with the cooperation, collaboration, and trust that are critical to maximizing potential.

In roughly eighteen months, a significant part of that company had turned over.

Today, many businesses have a toxic influence on the well-being of their team members and their families. We lament what is happening to the youth of the world, yet we in business persist in sending people home broken, and there they struggle with their marriages and with parenting. Many business leaders think that people should feel lucky to have a job. But the stark fact is the way we treat people at work affects the way they feel and how they treat the people in their life.[21]

"Train people well enough so they can leave, treat them well enough so they don't want to."

—Richard Branson

Trust and engagement are not competencies and skills we extract out of people. They are not items you can pull off the grocery shelf for the company picnic. Trust and engagement are not moves to make, ideas you can spin, or weapons you can carry. *Trust* is a condition owned by the one who does the trusting. The trustee has to earn trust through authenticity and integrity in every moment of the relationship. Similarly, we don't *engage* someone, they engage on their own. We can influence and inspire. We can give them great reasons to engage or feel engaged, but it's condescending to suggest that you hold the keys to another's engagement. Engaging your people isn't something you do to them; it's a consequence of what you do for them and with them.

One VP I worked with greeted me each time we met with what you might call the "silent- forehead treatment." He was so buried headfirst in e-mail and social media that he wouldn't even greet me. I didn't feel respected or valued, and consequently, that seemingly small act eroded my trust.

---

21   Bob Chapman and Raj Sisodia, *Everybody Matters: The Extraordinary Power of Caring for Your People Like Family* (New York: Penguin, 2015).

Jim Snider, on the other hand, earned my trust with his consistent focus on success both through and with me. He took accountability for every one of his leaders and the people on their teams. From day one, Jim was focused on getting the job done, but he knew that success was the result of trusting relationships. We spoke live at least once per week. We met in person for several hours approximately every eight weeks. He began each conversation asking, "How are you? How is your wife; your children? Are you happy? What's working in the job for you? What are you challenged with? How can I help? What's the larger goal? What can *we* do to achieve that goal?" Then he would ask perhaps the most beautiful question a leader can ask: "How can I do a better job of leading and developing you?"

If you're trustworthy, caring, and committed to your people and the work, then you will all be so engaged doing great work and having fun, that you won't have time to measure and analyze trust and engagement. We need to let the brain do what it does and let the heart do what it does. Share your best selves with positive intentions and integrity toward others, and watch the trust and engagement issues go away.

> *"Crisis of meaning occurs when our accumulation of knowledge far exceeds the tempering effect of our values."*
>
> —Sir John Whitmore, *Coaching for Performance*

We engage others and build trust when we put basic values and humanity over money, power, and technology. We engage others when we connect with what unites us all: the heart. When we first align our hearts and *then* our heads, we can do amazing things. We can't think or strategize our way into trust. Leaders cannot get full buy-in and commitment to a vision unless they demonstrate sincerity for their cause. Steve Jobs is notorious for having a tough personality, but he cared fiercely about what he was doing, and he knew he needed people to accomplish his audacious goals. Even Jobs, when asked about technology, discussed its value in empowering people—colleagues and customers. He said, "It's not a faith in technology. It's faith in people." He went on to explain, "Technology is nothing. What's important is that you have a faith in people, that they're basically good and smart, and if you give them tools, they'll do wonderful things with them."[22]

There is no shortage of data out there on workplace dissatisfaction and opportunities for improvement. In spite of the multibillion-dollar organizational leadership, culture, and coaching industry we've built, trust and engagement metrics have been consistently low for over ten years. Roughly seven out of ten employees are disengaged in their work and untrusting of their leaders—an emotional, spiritual, and financially disturbing statistic.[23] People are unhappy at work. Everyone loses. What I find much more interesting (I suspect you do, too) is the question of what can be done about it. How can we be happier at work? How can we be more trustworthy, engaging, and empowering leaders and coaches?

Caring is the answer. If people do not feel cared about, they won't trust. If they don't trust, they won't put their heart and soul into the cause, the team, the work, or the art. The relationship with one another, the boss, the team, and the organization take precedence over everything else. George E. Vaillant, director of the Grant Study, a fifty-year study of over 250 physically and mentally healthy adult males and author of *Triumphs of Experience: The Men of the Harvard*

---

22   Jeff Goodell, "Steve Jobs in 1994: The Rolling Stone Interview," *Rolling Stone*, January 17, 2011, http://www.rollingstone.com/culture/news/steve-jobs-in-1994-the-rolling-stone-interview-20110117.

23   "State of the American Manager," Gallup, http://www.gallup.com/Search/Default.aspx?s=&p=1&q=State+of+the+American+Manager&b=Go.

Grant Study, concluded that "Warmth of relationships throughout life have the greatest positive impact on 'life satisfaction.' Happiness is love. Full stop." My unscientific view is that women are generally better at relationships then men, so I am guessing that if 250 women were studied the same way, warm and loving relationships would win the day in that study as well.

Relationships matter. Feelings matter. Human connections matter. Cultures benefit from developing an awareness of how people engage. Respect, compassion, and kindness are all cousin words to *love* and *caring*. The specific definitions people give them are irrelevant. The point is to embrace the essence of what giving heed to these words means. And I don't mean lollipops and stuffed animals. I mean a general concern for the well-being and care of others. Leave out the words and labels; simply put the "concern-for-the-well-being-of-others" lens over your eyes. You will change relationships, teams, cultures, and the world.

> *"Changing an organization, a company, a country—or a world—begins with the simple step of changing yourself,"*
>
> —Tony Robbins, *Awaken the Giant Within*

Fortune's annual list of top companies to work for is one place to witness grace at work. Many of these companies appear on that list every year, and it's not by accident; clearly there's something different about the way that they operate. One that stands out to me is Wegmans, my hometown grocery store (which has expanded throughout the East Coast). Wegmans has appeared on the list every year since its inception. On their website, this is the first item on their list of values: "We care about the well-being and success of every person."[24]

The best companies make caring a priority: caring about their people and their valued customers. They develop a battle strategy in the marketplace and think deep into the future to what they want to be, what their corporate identity is, and what they want to contribute. The best companies have a Caring-Warrior spirit because they concern themselves with being the kind of company people want to work for.

---

24   Wegmans, https://www.wegmans.com/webapp/wcs/stores/servlet/CategoryDisplay?storeId=10052&identifier=CATEGORY_2441#believe.

CHAPTER 8

INSPIRE

"Culture eats strategy for breakfast."

—Peter Drucker

Experience Life magazine arrived in my mailbox one day. I thought it was great, but I hadn't filled out any subscription cards or been to their website, so I assumed it was a mistake and this would be the only time it would come. I absolutely loved the magazine and read it cover to cover. It was right in my sweet spot: everything from fitness to spirituality to healthy eating and living to self-development. I loved the positive themes: authenticity, happiness, and wellness. It kept coming once a month. My favorite part was an inspirational letter/message from the CEO, Bahram Akradi. I had no idea who he was, but I loved what he had to say. I felt as though each month he was writing a note meant just for me to help me live a better life. Then, the magazine stopped coming.

Many years later, my wife became a fitness instructor at Lifetime Fitness. These are beautifully kept and motivational health clubs, unlike any I have ever seen. She loves the company and regularly talks about the mission and culture as lived, not just words in a frame on the executive office wall. Lifetime cares about the health and well-being of their employees. Lifetime Fitness's mission is to provide entertaining, educational, friendly, inviting, functional, and innovative experiences that improve the health and wellness of others. They have a rigorous hiring process in order to only bring in competent leaders and professionals who are passionate about helping people to experience a healthier life.

Once hired, employees experience the mission played out in the culture, with continuous staff development, team building, health-themed competitions, special events, and good old-fashioned fun at work. The atmosphere in those clubs is contagious. Positive.

In 2011, Lifetime Fitness started the Lifetime Foundation, a program to inspire a healthier planet through partnerships with schools, providing education and activities. They treat people with respect, and their caring spirit translates to their customers and the positive culture of their facilities. One day not long ago, my wife said, "You have to see this note from Bahram, our CEO." I was blown away as I read a top leader in an organization speaking to his people with such vulnerability, appreciation, and respect. After complimenting individuals and the larger organization for specific achievements and efforts, he closed his note with, "I truly love you all, CEO—Bahram Akradi." How rare and beautiful is that? A CEO expressing love and appreciation for his people. Akradi lives what he writes and says. He is known to jump right in the middle of a group fitness class or take the microphone and lead a heart-thumping spin class. I would go through a brick wall for that kind of leader!

"Loyalty is earned and it stems from you," writes Nina Ojeda in *Inc.* magazine. Leaders of small and large organizations often fail to realize that they, *as leaders,* are the culture. Ojeda continues, "No matter the size of your company, maintaining a strong culture that YOU define is important for many reasons, including the optimization of productivity, and employee retention."[25] How top leaders behave, communicate, and treat people dictates the efficacy and performance of the culture. Many don't get it. Daina Trout, cofounder and CEO of Health-Ade Kombucha does. She believes that employees need to feel connected to the organization, beginning with the leader and playing out in regular conversations defining expectations of what success looks like. Leaders have to care enough to have those conversations. The point isn't using words such as "love" or telling people "I care!" Loyalty to the mission and commitment to the work that needs to get done are inspired (or are not) by a leader's behavior.

In my role as head of training, I gathered and analyzed the results of many company-wide surveys and assessments. The written feedback was always more telling than the numbers. Comments for the top-ranked leaders regularly highlighted leader behaviors such as coaching and feedback, positivity, availability and willingness to help, and inspiration. The best leaders inspired their teams because they cared for their people not only in their words but also in their

---

25   Nina Ojeda, ""What the Best Leaders Do to Create a Great Company Culture," August 19, 2016, *Inc.*, http://www.inc.com/nina-ojeda/what-the-best-leaders-do-to-create-a-great-company-culture.html.

deeds. And in turn, employees would say, "I not only worked hard for myself, but I also wanted to do well for my boss."

Jeff Weiner, CEO of LinkedIn, discussed the value of caring in company culture during an interview with Oprah. He spoke of the importance of values—not just stating them superficially from the stage but living them. He said, "When we are encouraging people to be open about what's on their minds, we're encouraging them to do so in a constructive way that lifts the dialogue, that lifts people up rather than tears them down."[26]

Creating caring cultures in our work and in the world begins with each of us. Caring Warriors like Mark McDade, Eddie Williams, Daina Trout, Bahram Akradi, and Jeff Weiner are too rare. Why shouldn't we expect our leaders to care more, to build up rather than tear down? Why don't we expect this of ourselves as leaders? Transforming a small or large culture is an inside-out job, meaning it begins with you, with me, the individual.

Believing you can fix cultures with an expensive, cookie-cutter program you buy is like going to a five-star Italian restaurant and eating two baskets of bread before your entrée comes. You're wasting your appetite on the wrong thing. Your purpose and your people are the entrée and the wine. And save some room for the dessert, which is the creativity and performance results you get from simply caring. Don't spend your time, money, and attention on the bread basket and miss the good stuff—your people. Talk with them. Find out how people feel on every team and at every level. Conduct focus groups or "fire-side chats" with your people. Share the vision. Share the problems, the solutions. Share the work. Share the experience and success. Share the fulfillment.

---

26   "CEO Jeff Weiner Shares the 6 Core Values at LinkedIn," SuperSoul.TV, http://www.supersoul.tv/supersoul-sunday/ceo-jeff-weiner-shares-6-core-values-linkedin.

Caring-Warrior companies, teams, and leaders say, "We share it!"

W.E. S.H.A.R.E. I.T.

W: WILL

Goodwill. Commit to be a beacon of light and possibility in the spirit of serving and benefiting others. Chasing money and short-term bragging rights will fall short of your culture's potential. Play the long game with a little more love. Be the change, be the culture you want to see.

E: EXPECTATION

Maintain a positive belief in the potential of the people you've either hired or who you share accountability with. Set a high bar for yourself, and lead by example. Resist the negativity in your head and in conversation with others; your culture, performance, and satisfaction never improve that way. Someone has to expect amazing progress and growth for everyone. Why shouldn't that be you? Is it you? Your beliefs become your reality and the outcomes of your organization.

S: SAFE

Fiercely guard the emotional, spiritual, and intellectual safety of your culture. Don't kid yourself—everything is personal. In order to contribute their very best, people need to feel safe. Their first concern, as we've learned, is trust. Are you trustworthy? Care for yourself by caring for others. Safeguard humanity.

H: HAPPINESS

What's it all worth, if you and the people around you—your teams, colleagues, and customers—aren't happy? Please decide to be more kind, caring, and happy. Caring and happiness work incredibly well together. Make someone else a little happier today. I promise you'll feel great about it.

A: AWARENESS

Our lives have a time limit. We do not know what that limit is. Wake up to what is now. Living and loving yourself, your loved ones, and the people you work with is what's happening *now*. We do not know if we'll have another chance when we say, "see you later," or "take care." Be grateful for what you have, for the freedoms and opportunities you enjoy. See those opportunities. See yourself. See others. Awareness is being alive and awake right now.

R: RECOGNIZE

Recognize and reward the people in your life. Let them know that what they do matters to you and to the big picture, the goals. We all want to matter, and we want to be told so. Validate and encourage by recognizing people. Don't miss opportunities to reinforce right effort in yourself and others.

E: EDUCATE

Human beings are wired for growth and learning. We atrophy and weaken in the absence of growth. Idle, understimulated minds will grow restless and unfulfilled. Invest in your own learning and growth, and support it in those around you. *Have a mentor and be a mentor.* I have been blessed with mentors at every turn in my life. Open your

eyes to the learning and growth that await you. Then teach others.
Lift one another up by always
striving to be a better version of
yourself, and help others do the
same.

> **HAVE A MENTOR AND BE A MENTOR.**

I: INTEGRITY

Stand for something. Develop a creed, a code of how you, your
teams, and your organizations want to relate to the world—how
you will contribute. Then hold yourself accountable for living up to
it. We begin a negative spiral individually and collectively when we
don't maintain our integrity. Breaking with our integrity and making
mistakes is part of being human, but keep striving to be better. Be
proud of who you are and who you are becoming. Inspire others by
sharing your very best.

T: TRUTH

The truth needs no defense—the truth simply *is*. The truth will set
you free.

TAKE UP YOUR SWORD

> "People say that what we're all seeking is a meaning for life.
> I don't think that's what we're really seeking. I think that
> what we're seeking is an experience of being alive, so that
> our life experiences on the purely physical plane will have
> resonances with our own innermost being and reality, so
> that we actually feel the rapture of being alive."
> —Joseph Campbell, *The Power of Myth*

BOSTON-STRONG CARING WARRIORS

With her Irish brogue, Toni Dunleavy asked, "Have you ever taught
tae kwon do to a boy with Down syndrome?"

Tom responded, "No, Mrs. Dunleavy, I haven't, but I will teach your son."

That day, Tom and Toni decided that because of her son John's challenges, he (eight years old) and his brother Michael (five) would take private lessons with Tom so he could focus all of his attention on them.

Tom DeFranzo is a special man. I know because he was my college roommate at Penn State, and he remains one of my dearest friends today. Tom was an exceptional and disciplined student during school. Tom is a person who knows who he is; he knows what his priorities are, and he puts all his focus on them. Tom went to class, studied methodically, hung out with me and a few other friends, and practiced martial arts. Our apartment was full of martial-arts weaponry. Like a true martial artist would, he treated every item with great care.

Malden, Massachusetts, where Tom grew up, has a Boston toughness about it. Tom is an interesting blend of tough and protective, yet sensitive and caring. He'd be the first guy to jump into a fight to protect a friend, and he'd be right there with you at a movie like *Rudy*, bawling his eyes out. Wiping his eyes, he'd say something like, "Oh my gaaawwwd, TJ. That movie's a teah-jerkuh!" Tom is a strong and Caring Warrior of the first order.

We lost touch for quite a few years. When we caught back up on a three-hour phone conversation, Tom said, "I have to tell you about the Dunleavy boys. They changed my life."

Day one, private lesson. 1998: "Sir, I'm already a black belt, but I haven't told anyone. I'm just here to practice my moves," said Michael, the five-year-old. John jumped in with his two cents, but because of his Down syndrome, his words were very hard to understand. Michael translated for his older brother and right away demonstrated a protective and loving role with John. Michael was younger, but he was John's big brother. These boys became little brothers to Tom as he met with them privately, twice every week for four years. They loved their tae kwon do lessons together, and they loved "Sir," their title for their teacher. Toni would tell Tom how she would hear noises coming from their shared bedroom at night. Peeking through the door, she saw Michael helping John with his moves. Tom fell in love with those boys and the entire Dunleavy family.

May 2002: Michael and John were progressing toward their black belts. They would likely have them that calendar year. Yet feisty and vibrant Michael, now nine, was having some issues with hearing and vision. Toni told Tom that he would tilt his head in an odd way when he spoke. That same month, Toni informed Tom that Michael had been diagnosed with an inoperable brain tumor. It was unlikely that Michael would survive.

Devastated beyond imagination, the Dunleavys decided that they would pray for a miracle and do their very best to keep Michael's (and John's) life as normal and happy as possible. And so, every Tuesday and Thursday (planned around his chemo and radiation treatments), Michael and John continued their cherished lessons with "Sir." Michael struggled more and more with balance and endurance, but like a true warrior, he kept fighting. When Tom asked Michael if he needed a break, he would respond, "Sir, I don't need a break. I need to earn my black belt."

Michael died on October 28.

Tom joined Michael's father, Gerry, on the altar to give Michael's eulogy.

Tom spoke of Michael's determination and spirit. He spoke of Michael's character and love for his brother John, of how John was Michael's translator and guardian. In tears, Tom told everyone that Michael had been *his* teacher, not the other way around. Michael had taught him about living.

The Boston marathon is run in April each year. Training in the bitter cold of the Northeast is often a deal breaker for would-be runners. Although he'd never been a runner, Tom decided to run in honor of Michael and raise money for the Michael Dunleavy Foundation.[27] The foundation was started by Michael's parents and focuses on childhood cancers and brain-tumor research, as well as treatment and assistance for children and families afflicted with this illness.

WWW.MICHAELDUNLEAVY.COM/FOUNDATION

WWW.MICHAELDUNLEAVY.COM/DONATIONS

Tom had five months to train in the cold Boston winter for his very first marathon. Many of his training runs ended with the soles of his sneakers completely frozen.

April 2003: The day of the race, Tom wore white athletic tape on his wrist with Michael's initials, MJD, on it. The big, Irish Dunleavy family gave Tom a shirt with their handprints traced on the back for an "extra push." Tom felt it. The muscular, 220-pound tae kwon do instructor completed the Boston Marathon for the next three years, carrying Michael's spirit with him every time.

---

27   Michael Dunleavy Foundation, http://www.michaeldunleavy.com/index.htm.

The third would be Tom's last time doing the race. Less than an hour into it, a runner in front of him dropped a bottle of Gatorade on the road. Tom tripped over it and went down hard on the pavement. He had broken his left foot, although he didn't know it at the time. He tried to walk off the pain. He wondered if he could make it. Hobbling down Heartbreak Hill was brutally painful. He looked down at the "MJD" on his wrist and thought about the Dunleavy family and their handprints on his back. He thought about Michael's fighting Irish spirit. He remembered all the lessons with the brothers. He kept going.

As Tom crossed the finish line, he got right into an ambulance to go to the hospital because of his foot. He burst into tears, remembering the last time he saw Michael in the hospital. Michael reached out to hug Tom, tubes everywhere, from under his beloved Red Sox blanket. As they hugged, Tom slipped the black belt around Michael's waist.

The Dunleavys later told Tom that Michael's last words were, "Take care of John."

Postscript

The Dunleavys miss their boy,
but they have a happy and vibrant family.

Tom's efforts have raised over $100,000
for the Michael Dunleavy Foundation.

In 2016, Tom rowed a 10K at his martial-arts
school to raise more money.

Tom awards one tae kwon do student each year
with the Michael Dunleavy Award.

John and Tom are best friends—brothers.

Michael and Tom in 2002, the year he passed away.

John and Tom at a Boston Bruins game, 2016.

*"They say in every life. They say the rain must fall.
Just like pouring rain. Make it rain. Make it rain.
Love, love, love is sunshine."*

—James Taylor, "Shower the People"

GEORGE BAILEY MOMENTS

I love the film *It's a Wonderful Life*, starring Jimmy Stewart. At a crucial breaking point in George's life, he has the opportunity to see what impact he had on the people in his life and on his community. George says, "I wish I'd never been born." Clarence, an angel, shows George the less-*wonderful* reality others would have experienced had George never existed—a front-row look at the what-if scenario. George is given the gift of seeing that he matters, that his life has meaning because of the impact he has had on others. Clarence tells George, "Each man's life touches so many other lives. When he isn't around he leaves an awful hole, doesn't he?"

Caring Warriors are awake and aware that they have the power to positively influence and inspire others, and they choose to do it. A Caring Warrior takes up the sword to make life better for everyone. A Caring Warrior need not be perfect or invincible, just willing to try—to keep fighting.

CARING-WARRIOR BATTLES WON, LARGE AND SMALL

Josh Yandt changed a school and his life by caring enough to open the door for others. One act of kindness can change the world.

Ashley, the new manager, cared enough to change herself in order to have positive influence and change her team, and their results, for the better.

Garrett Miller took up the sword of personal excellence to inspire his school and represent his country in world competition.

Coach Ron Hunter took off his own shoes and put a new pair on the feet of millions of children.

Coach Mike Haugh taught and coached countless young men about true strength and honor.

Bill Loftus showed a new manager (me) what true team spirit and the meaning of Christmas is.

Mendy Shaw Ringer brought her leadership magic and warmth to influence and make a positive impact. Many of her direct reports have gone on to become Caring Warriors—leaders in other organizations who *care it forward*.

Eddie Williams launched my leadership career (many others too), teaching the ever-important philosophy of "putting your people first."

Mark McDade cared enough to lead from the heart with intention. Many former colleagues say that working with Mark in that organization was the happiest and most engaged they've been in their careers.

Charlie Symington showed me a kindness when I needed it most.

Navy SEALs (and all our servicewomen and men) choose to put themselves in harm's way in order to protect and defend others. They honor us with their caring courage and sacrifice.

Bahram Akradi leads with love and brings a special breed of health and wellness to others in his organization and into the world.

Tom DeFranzo teaches young people (future leaders) about discipline and character: the enduring, loving, and Caring-Warrior spirit of Michael Dunleavy.

We have crucial moments in the story of our lives, as heroes, when we're "up against it." These moments can be large or small, personal or professional. The fate of the universe need not rest in the balance for us to be heroic. We can be heroic with small commitments to be a little more kind and caring to ourselves and others. Each of these moments represents a new fight, a new battle for the Caring Warrior. We simply have to choose. We can choose to be defeated by our enemies: fear, negativity, or selfishness. Or we can choose to care enough to fight. Choosing the fight is the more difficult path, but I'll remind you again of Paulo Coelho's words in *The Alchemist*: "There is only one way to learn. It's through action." We find ourselves in the wounds we suffer while fighting on the battlegrounds of life. The Caring Warrior discovers *meaning* and truth fighting for love. We live when we love.

Your warrior's call: Awaken and own your life. Influence others by giving. Inspire your culture and the world by sharing. Shine your light into the dark places with your caring heart.

The fight continues, Caring Warrior. We need you.

Pick up your sword.

> *"What we do in life, echoes in eternity."*
>
> —Maximus, *Gladiator*

SUMMARY

- Caring Warriors
    - care about people first, then products and profits;
    - are sincere, real;
    - connect people to one another;
    - develop and support growth for those they influence; and
    - possess a caring heart.
- Everyone matters.
- Relationships matter.
- Trust and engagement are responses to trustworthy and caring behavior.
- Sharing inspires.
- Love yourself.
- Love others.

EXERCISES

Describe in detail the cultures in which you function and the role(s) you play in those cultures.

- **social** (circle of family and friends, tribe, club, peers, events, etc.)

- **community** (where you live)

- **school** (where your children go or where you go if you're a student)

- **work** (your organization, industry, or business)

- **world** (your generation, religion, spiritual affiliation, or political identity)

1. What works for you? What about your culture/environment do you agree with and believe in?

2. Are your basic values and beliefs in alignment with this culture and the people in it? If yes, explain. If no, explain: What about this culture does not work for you? Describe in detail the mismatch between who you are and the culture that isn't working for you.

3. What influence do you have in each of the roles you play? Are you part of the solution or the problem? Are you influencing and inspiring the people around you?

4. What relationship or situation is challenging you right now that you need to confront as soon as possible? What is your intention? What is the best possible outcome you can expect? How can you bring your best self to that situation?

5. Who and what inspire you? How do you feel when you are inspired? What do you do?

6. What moves you to passion/emotion? Under what conditions do you feel most connected to and caring for others? What are you thinking, feeling, and doing in those moments? What truths are revealed to you about yourself and the cultures in which you function?

7. Are the people you surround yourself with lifting you up or pulling you down? Are you lifting those around you up or pulling them down?

8. What do you need to apologize for? To whom do you need to apologize?

9. Disregarding regrets and disappointments of the past and anxiety about the future, what do you know in your heart would give you the greatest sense of fulfillment as it relates to your place in the cultures you choose or find yourself in?

10. Do you care for yourself? Do you care for others?

11. In what ways can you, today, become a Caring Warrior? How will you feel? What positive changes in your culture and relationships would you experience by making that positive change?

12. Who in your life needs to know the changes you want to make?

Pick up your sword.

RESOURCES

BOOKS/ARTICLES

- *Everybody Matters: The Extraordinary Power of Caring for Your People Like Family,* Bob Chapman and Raj Sisodia
- *The Power of Myth,* Joseph Campbell
- *Triumphs of Experience: The Men of the Harvard Grant Study,* George E. Vaillant
- *Awaken the Giant Within,* Tony Robbins
- *Coaching for Performance,* Sir John Whitmore
- Jeff Goodell, "Steve Jobs in 1994: The Rolling Stone Interview," *Rolling Stone,* January 17, 2011, http://www.rollingstone.com/culture/news/steve-jobs-in-1994-the-rolling-stone-interview-20110117?utm_source=email.
- G.R.A.C.E. at WORK INSTITUTE, Eric de Nijs, EdD, http://www.gracewins.co/dr-eric-de-nijs.html
- "Building the High-Performance Workforce," Corporate Leadership Council, 2002, http://docplayer.net/5496089-Building-the-high-performance-workforce-a-quantitative-analysis-of-the-effectiveness-of-performance-management-strategies.html
- "Wegmans Food Markets, Inc.: An Overview," Wegmans, https://www.wegmans.com/webapp/wcs/stores/servlet/CategoryDisplay?storeId=10052&identifier=CATEGORY_2441#believe
- *Experience Life* magazine, https://experiencelife.com/

SONGS/FILMS

- "Shower the People," James Taylor
- *Gladiator*

ACKNOWLEDGMENTS

My desire to be a Caring Warrior is only possible through the love I am blessed to have in my life, which begins with Molly, my wife. Very little would make sense to me in this life without you and the life we have with our children: Meghan, Abby, Patrick, and Henry. To my immediate family—you've propped me up and jumped into the good fight with me. My love and appreciation for each of you: Mom, Kerry Jones, Clare Stich, Mike Jones, Larry and Nancy Waldron, Mig and Kiki Boscan, Pete and Courtney Waldron, and Michael Sansez.

Dad and Joe, I miss you both every day. In your own unique ways, you were both Caring Warriors.

My best bros Leigh J. Pope, Joe Renda, and Tom DeFranzo—you've kept me going and believing that I could do this and encouraging me to "make a difference." Several friends and former colleagues have been constant cheerleaders—original believers and motivators for the Caring Warrior: Mike Ferrara, Matt Moyer, Jen Murawski, Kim Stern, Claudia Raya, Julie Hunsicker, Donna Buschick, Mike Kirschner, Ken Livingston, and Ray Rodriguez.

My thanks and respect to the colleagues I've mentioned in the book: Mark McDade, Eddie Williams, Bill Loftus, Jim Snider, and Mendy Shaw. Thank you to the many students, athletes, team members, trainees, and colleagues, both for the experiences and for being a part of my life's story. I also want to mention former colleagues whose names were changed or omitted. I am grateful for the life lessons you've taught me and the motivation you've given me to get better.

I'd like to acknowledge the Caring-Warrior teachers, educators, coaches, and mentors who touched my life and changed its course and direction for the positive when I was a student and young teacher. My love and gratitude to Mike Haugh, Coach Girolmo, Gary Groth, Sandy Syzmanski, Father Joe, Father John, Lee Giannone, Mr. Pillagalli, Helen Catherine White, Tom Barna, and Nick Coggins.

Helen Douthat—thank you for helping me wake up. You rooted for me and the promise of a Caring Warrior. You helped more than you'll ever know. You've been a blessing. I'd also like to thank the two best doctors a person could have: Dr. Charlene Connors and Dr. Martha Boone.

Charlie Symington - best neighbor a guy could have.

Steve Cesari—your book, *Clarity*, kick-started my belief that I could do this. Your guidance, wisdom, and friendship helped to make it possible. Thank you to Darren Ho for guiding me through my deep cliff dive out of my corporate career.

Thank you, Jenny Tripp, for helping me separate the good stuff from the bad stuff. You are definitely in the "good-stuff" category.

Thank you to Tom Kukla and Loy Day for having an early look at the manuscript. Your insights and feedback were invaluable.

To my friends and team at Advantage Media: Adam Witty, Rusty Shelton, Patti Boysen, Alison Morse, Shelby Sledge, Ben Coppel, Kirby Andersen, Eland Mann, Helen Harris, Peter Berry, Jonna Palmer, Allison Looney, Paige McKinney, Paige Velasquez, Sara Pence, Amy Jordan, Brandon Procell, Shelby Janner, Steven Janiak, George Stevens, Megan Elger, and Katie Biondo. You've kept me semi-sane and have been a great team to work with. Thank you.

ABOUT THE AUTHOR

TJ is an author, speaker, and leadership crusader. TJ has a diverse background with experience as an athlete, actor-singer, teacher, high school and college coach, business leader, and head of training and development. He studied communications and speech at the Pennsylvania State University and holds a graduate degree and teaching certification in English, speech, and drama. TJ holds several professional certifications in leadership, team development, and executive coaching. Drawing from twenty years of real-world corporate experience and awards in sales, leadership, and organizational excellence, TJ teaches emerging leaders, teams, and companies how to reach new heights of fulfillment and performance. His teaching, speaking, and coaching engagements are always fun, unique, and high impact.

TJ lives in Atlanta, GA, with his wife and four children where he can be found hiking, coaching his sons in baseball, attending his daughter's chorus concerts, and happily carrying the warrior's sword.

TJJonesLeadership.com
linkedin.com/in/TimothyJJones1
twitter.com/CaringWarriorTJ

TAKE UP YOUR SWORD.
For more resources and to take the
Positive Influence Assessment,
visit TJJonesLeadership.com.

CARING IS THE HEART OF LEADERSHIP.
OWN IT. GIVE IT. SHARE IT.

AWAKEN Your Inner Warrior

Awaken to YOU, know what you are fighting for. Be More. Own it. Care for you.

INFLUENCE Your Tribe

Influence others. Connect. Empower. Develop. Motivate. Care to lead.

INSPIRE Your Culture

Inspire action and creativity. Integrate. Collaborate. Innovate. Care for your culture.

YOU

YOUR TEAM

YOUR ORGANIZATION

Printed in the USA
CPSIA information can be obtained
at www.ICGtesting.com
JSHW051552111023
50048JS00020B/924